Table of Contents

CONTEMPORARY'S

The GED Essay

WRITING SKILLS TO PASS THE TEST

ELLEN C. FRECHETTE

Project Editor

Pat Fiene

CONTEMPORARY BOOKS

a division of NTC/CONTEMPORARY PUBLISHING GROUP
Lincolnwood, Illinois USA

Library of Congress Cataloging-in-Publication Data

Frechette, Ellen.
    The GED essay / Ellen Frechette.
       p.   cm.
    ISBN 0-8092-3772-5
    1. General educational development tests—Study guides.   2. Essay—
Study and teaching (Secondary)   3. English language—Composition
and exercises—Study guides.   I. Title.
LB3060.33.G45F64   1993
808′.042′076—dc20

                                                                 93-14162
                                                                 CIP

ISBN: 0-8092-3772-5

Published by Contemporary Books,
a division of NTC/Contemporary Publishing Group, Inc.,
4255 West Touhy Avenue,
Lincolnwood (Chicago), Illinois 60646-1975 U.S.A.
Manufactured in the United States of America.
8 9 0 CU 15 14 13 12 11 10

Editorial Director
Mark Boone

Editorial
Lisa Black
Lynn McEwan
Scott Gutmann
Gigi Grajdura
Caren Van Slyke

Editorial Assistant
Maggie McCann

Editorial Production Manager
Norma Fioretti

Production Editor
Thomas D. Scharf

Cover Design
Georgene Sainati

Art & Production
Julie Smith
Sue Springston

Typography
Ellen Kollmon

Front cover computer-generated graphic by Communi-K

An important part of preparing for the essay portion of the GED Writing Skills Test is understanding what you'll be asked to do on the test. In the past, you may have completed many different kinds of writing tasks—writing a letter to apply for a job, writing directions to your home, or writing a note to a child's teacher. Each of these writing tasks required something different from you. Writing an essay for the GED has its own requirements too.

The GED Essay: Writing Skills to Pass the Test begins by telling you exactly what is required for success on the GED essay. You'll get a chance to

- analyze sample GED essay topics
- study examples of effective GED essays
- learn what the evaluators of your essay will be looking for when they score your paper
- practice different strategies for planning a GED essay
- use the process approach to write a GED essay

Armed with a knowledge of the requirements of the test and strategies for success, you'll be well prepared for the essay portion of the GED Writing Skills Test.

As you work through *The GED Essay: Writing Skills to Pass the Test*, look for these features:

- **GED-style topics**—practice topics written in the style of actual GED essay topics
- **Writing Checklists**—lists of questions that you can use to evaluate your own work
- **Practice with a Partner**—writing and evaluation activities to do with a friend or family member
- **Writer's Workshop**—a wealth of handouts with activities to sharpen your GED writing skills
- **Test Tips**—strategies for succeeding on the Writing Skills Test
- **Answer Key**—clearly explained answers that allow you to evaluate your own work

The skills you acquire as you work through this book will help you when you take the test—and in other future writing tasks as well. Good luck on the GED Writing Skills Test!

The Editors

THE WRITING PROCESS

☑ PREWRITING

1. Understand the test
   - The GED and the writing process
   - GED essay evaluation
   - The essay form
2. Analyze the topic
3. Generate ideas and make a plan

☐ DRAFTING

4. Write the essay

☐ REVISING

5. Read over and improve the essay
6. Use good test-taking strategies

WHAT WILL I BE ASKED TO DO ON THE TEST?

The essay portion of the GED Writing Skills Test asks you to (circle one)

(a) write for 45 minutes and produce a perfect essay on an unfamiliar topic.

(b) take 45 minutes to plan, write, and revise a first draft of an essay on a familiar topic.

For the Writing Skills Test, you'll be asked to use the **writing process** to produce an essay within a 45-minute time limit. In other words, you'll be given 45 minutes to plan, write, and revise an essay. A first draft, not a perfect piece of writing, is all that's required. Here's a quick look at what the writing process is and how it's covered in this book:

Prewriting

Chapters 1–3

- Understand the test
- Analyze the topic
- Generate ideas and plan

Drafting

Chapter 4

- Use the plan to write an introduction, body, and conclusion

Revising

Chapters 5–6

- Read over the essay and make changes
- Correct grammar and spelling mistakes
- Use good test-taking strategies

> **TEST TIP**
>
> You're allowed to use scratch paper when you take the test. Use it to jot down notes and to plan your essay.

You may be interested to know that some of the least effective GED essays are written by people who spend the entire 45 minutes writing. In this book, you'll learn to *think* first, *write* second. If you take time to think and plan, your essay will be better organized and easier to understand.

WHAT WILL THE TOPIC BE?

The GED essay topics are subjects that all adults are familiar with. You *won't* be asked to write about a topic like this:

- What are the countries that made up the former Soviet Union, and what type of government has each established?

The topic above wouldn't appear on the test because people would need specialized knowledge to write about it. Instead, you might be asked to write about a topic like this:

- What are the effects of the automobile on modern life?

Notice that you don't need specialized knowledge to write about the topic. Even if you have never driven or owned an automobile, you still could be expected to have some ideas about how cars affect our lives.

For example, you may have been in traffic jams or seen TV news stories about air pollution. Common sense also tells you that, in general, automobiles get people where they want to go more quickly than walking. These are the kinds of ideas that you could use in your essay.

Here are some more possible topics. Take a couple of minutes to jot down one or two ideas that could be included in essays on these subjects.

▶ ways in which airplanes have changed our lives

_____

_____

▶ advantages of getting a good education

_____

_____

▶ characteristics of a good friend

_____

_____

▶ reasons why people should stop smoking

_____

_____

You may think you don't have enough ideas to write about these topics, but you probably do. The trick is to get your thoughts flowing. This book has many strategies to help you do just that.

TEST TIP
There is no way to study for the GED essay topic, nor will you need to. The best preparation is writing, writing, and more writing.

See the Writer's Workshop handout "Finding the Writer Within," page 81.

PART ONE

■ **The steps below are directions from the actual GED Writing Skills Test, but they are not in order. Decide what stage of the writing process each step belongs in. On the blank line, write *P* if the step is in the prewriting stage, *D* if it belongs in the drafting stage, or *R* if it is in the revising stage. You may use a letter more than once.**

—— Write your essay on the lined pages of the separate answer sheet.

—— Use scratch paper to make any notes.

—— Read carefully the directions and the essay topic given below.

—— Check your paragraphs, sentence structure, spelling, punctuation, capitalization, and usage, and make any necessary corrections.

—— Plan your essay carefully before you write.

—— Read carefully what you have written and make any changes that will improve your essay.

PART TWO

■ **Circle the letter of each subject that could be a GED essay topic. If you're not sure about a topic, ask yourself whether a person would need specialized knowledge to write about it.**

(a) What do you think are the characteristics of a good job?

(b) What are the causes of a volcanic eruption?

(c) What are some reasons why so few people vote?

(d) What qualities does it take to be a good parent?

(e) What major civil rights legislation was enacted in the 1960s?

(f) What were the main effects of the Great Depression?

Check your answers on page 75.

The evaluation of your GED essay will be based on (circle one)

(a) the number of mistakes it contains and pages it fills.

(b) its overall effectiveness—how well you explain and support your main idea.

Your essay will be evaluated according to how effective it is overall. An effective essay is easy to understand. It clearly presents a **main idea**—a central point or points that the writer wants to make.

Look at the paragraphs below. The writers were asked to answer the question *Do you think a four-day work week would be better than our current five-day system?* Think about the overall effectiveness of each paragraph. On the blank lines, write down whether or not you can understand the writer's main point. Then write down why you answered the way you did.

HINT: Ask yourself, Does the writer think the four-day work week is a good idea, and does the writer tell why?

I would like a four-day work week. It is not an excellent idea. People throughout the country would not like this plan. Would this be good for America? It is an interesting idea.

_____
_____
_____
_____
_____

A four-day work weak. It not decided. Werkers shood more producing. The tim was here so that to put labor first. What are needs of the peopol? More pay at greater hour—is it fare?

_____
_____
_____
_____
_____

The United states should have a four-day work week becuase more leisure time would make people more productive. Americans would work harder to get more time off.

_____
_____
_____
_____
_____

Which paragraph did you think was the most effective? Most people would pick paragraph 3. Here's why.

- Paragraph 1 is completely free of mistakes in grammar and spelling. But being error-free doesn't make it an effective paragraph. The problem is that the paragraph doesn't have a clear main idea. The writer's central point—what he thinks about the four-day work week—isn't clear.

- The grammar and spelling problems in paragraph 2 make it difficult to read. In addition, the paragraph is hard to understand because it doesn't have a main idea. It's impossible to tell what central point or points the writer wants to make.

- Although paragraph 3 has some grammar and spelling mistakes, it's still easy to understand. Overall, the paragraph is effective because it has a clear main idea. It's easy to see what the writer thinks about the four-day work week. She's in favor of it because she believes it would make Americans more productive.

In the paragraphs above, correct grammar and spelling are important. However, a few mistakes don't matter. The same is true of the GED essay. The people who score your essay will be interested in how clearly you state and organize your ideas, not just in grammar and mechanical things like spelling, capitalization, and punctuation. Here are some general evaluation guidelines. You'll learn more about these criteria as you work through the book.

An effective essay	An ineffective essay
• presents a clear main idea	• does not present a clear main idea
• is well planned	• is not planned out
• has a logical structure	• lacks a clear structure
• offers support for ideas	• gives little or no support for ideas
• has few or no grammatical and spelling errors	• may have several or many grammatical and spelling errors

■ **Which paragraph in each pair is more effective? Use the criteria in the lists on page 6 to decide. Then circle the letter of the more effective paragraph.**

(1) Question: Should all citizens have the right to own a handgun?

(a) *People should be able to own guns if they want. But not if they are dangerous. Having guns is not a good idea. They protect people. They hurt.*

(b) *Guns should not be alowed in the homes of private citizens. Far to many accidents occur and statistics show that more innocent people than criminals die from handguns.*

(2) Question: What will our country's biggest problem be in the 21st century?

(a) *Out of all the possable problems America could face, pollution will be the biggest. For many years we have bin growing as an industrial nation with out taking care of our resources. Think of all the toxic waste that is poured into our lakes and rivers everyday. In the year 2000, we'll have to pay for all our growth.*

(b) *In the 21st century, America will be a leader worldwide in manufacturing high technology. There will be problems associated with this position. But we will still be number one in everything we do and this is what makes our country great. Even with our problems, we all can still say we are living the American dream.*

(3) Question: Do you like the age you are now, or would you rather be a different age? Why?

(a) *I'm twentey years old right now, but I'd rather ten. When your younger, you don't have all the cares and worries that adults have. Now I have to think about rent money, job security, my boyfriend. When I was ten, all I had to do was go to school and play all day.*

(b) *No matter what age you are, there are advantages and disadvantages. I am thirty-two years old, and I like my independence. However, I don't like the idea of hitting middle age. I hated being a teenager too. Being fifty might be cool because you'd be established.*

Check your answers on page 75.

See the Writer's Workshop handout "A Look at the GED Essay Scoring Guide," page 83.

The essay below was written in response to this topic:

Different people look for different qualities in a friend. Some people want friends whose interests are the same as their own. Others look for people who are easy to talk with. Still others look for people whom they admire.

Write an essay of about 200 words explaining the characteristics you think are important in a friend. Be specific and give examples showing what you mean.

The *introduction* lets readers know what the essay is about.

There are two qualities that I really value in a friend, and both of them are qualities I find in myself. The first one is loyalty. The second is a sense of humor. Without these two ingredients, a friendship is not worth keeping.

A good introduction tells readers the main idea of the essay.

The *body* explains and supports the main idea. Here, the writer gives a specific example to show what *loyalty* means to her.

Loyalty is more than kindness and generosity. It means sticking by a friend even when he or she is hard to be around. When I was going through my divorce, I was not a really happy person. But my best friends supported me and loved me anyway.

Another specific example supports the main idea.

And what good is a friendship if you can't laugh together? Life is too short to spend it always worrying about what will happen next. One thing I like the most about my friends is their ability to find humor in just about anything. Like the time I scratched my friend's car up, and he laughed instead of ~~screeming~~ screaming at me.

Occasional mistakes do not make the essay too difficult to read or understand.

Crossing out and adding are OK as long as the essay is still readable.

The *conclusion* sums up what the essay is about.

I think I'm a pretty loyal friend, and I think I have a great sense of humor. Maybe that's why these qualities are so important to me.

Think about the topic on page 8. Take several minutes to jot down ideas about what you might say in an essay on this topic. Then write a few sentences that tell what your main idea would be if you were writing this essay.

Jot down your ideas here.

Write your main idea on the lines below.

_____

_____

_____

Answers will vary.

At the end of each chapter in this book is a special activity called "Practice with a Partner." These activities give you opportunities to work with a classmate or friend as you prepare for the essay portion of the GED Writing Skills Test. By sharing your ideas and your writing with a partner, you'll both improve your skills.

Some helpful hints, called "Giving Constructive Criticism," are found in the Writer's Workshop handout on page 85. Use these hints whenever you and your partner share your writing. They will help you discuss the strong and weak points of your writing with each other.

For your first "partner practice," you and your partner should read the essay below. Following the essay are some students' comments about the essay's strengths and weaknesses. Talk about how the comments might be reworded to be more helpful. Then, using the guidelines on page 85, write your own, improved comments.

There are two things I appreciate in my friends. The first one is having fun. Lets face it, if you not having a good time at least sometimes, whats the point of having a freind anyway. When I go out, I like to hang, listen to music, play cards or just sit and talk. I never go to concerts or clubs because they are all so expensive. My friends like to do the same things. Thats why we're friends. When were not having fun, we can still be with each other like friends do.

Comments

"You didn't even finish the essay. You say that there are *two* things you like in a friend."

_____

"Ever heard of an apostrophe? You never use any."

_____

"I think the paper is good."

_____

THE WRITING PROCESS

☑ PREWRITING

1. Understand the test
2. Analyze the topic
   - Reading the background statement and instructions
   - Writing about causes and effects
   - Writing about advantages and disadvantages
   - Writing about characteristics
   - Writing your opinion
3. Generate ideas and make a plan

☐ DRAFTING

4. Write the essay

☐ REVISING

5. Read over and improve the essay
6. Use good test-taking strategies

Which of the following statements is most like a GED essay topic? (circle one)

(a) Write an essay about dropping out of school.

(b) Write an essay about why so many young people drop out of school.

The first topic asks you to write *anything* about dropping out of school. You could write a story about a friend who dropped out, about why dropping out is a bad idea, or about how many people drop out. A general topic like this one would *not* appear on the GED test.

The second topic above is more like a real GED topic. Notice that it gives you specific directions about writing your essay. It tells you to write about *why* young people drop out of school. In response to this topic, you couldn't write a story about a friend dropping out. Nor could you write about why it's a bad idea to drop out of school. Your essay must only discuss *why* young people drop out.

> A GED essay topic gives a general subject and specific instructions on what to write about the subject.

Take a look at the **form** of a GED essay topic:

All essay topics include a *background statement* like this one.

Background statements give information and ideas about a topic.

"It's a terrible shame that young people spend so much of their time staring at television. If we unplugged all the television sets, our children would grow up to be healthier, better educated, and more independent."

Do you agree or disagree with this statement? Write an essay of about 200 words presenting your point of view and supporting it with specific examples from your own experience or your observations of others.

All topics include *specific instructions* telling how to respond to the background statement.

All topics include this *200-word guideline*.

- The **background statement** is about kids watching TV.
- The **specific instructions** ask you to tell whether you agree or disagree with the statement, then to back up your opinion with examples.

EXERCISE 1

■ **For each topic below, circle the background statement and underline the specific instructions. Then, in your own words, explain what you're asked to write about.**

(1) "A good education is the most important thing in a person's life. Without it, health, happiness, and wealth are impossible."

Do you agree or disagree with this statement? Write an essay of about 200 words presenting your point of view and supporting it with specific examples from your own experience or your observations of others.

_____

(2) What qualities do you think make a good employer? Some people believe honesty is important; others believe that flexibility is.

Write an essay of about 200 words that identifies the qualities you think a good employer has, giving specific examples to back up your ideas.

_____

(3) Many state governments conduct lotteries, a form of legal gambling in which people pay for a ticket and hope that their numbers are selected in a random drawing. Some of the money collected goes to the winners; the rest is used for public needs such as schools and highways. What do you think are the effects of state lotteries on society? Write an essay of about 200 words stating and supporting your opinion.

_____

(4) It seems that more and more Americans are exercising and watching what they eat. What do you think is causing this "fitness kick"? Is it primarily concern with health, body image, or something else? Write an essay of about 200 words that tells the causes of the "fitness kick" and gives examples.

_____

Check your answers on page 75.

Read the topic at right. Which of these topics do the instructions say to write about?

(a) reasons why the computer has had such an impact on daily life

(b) the effects of the computer on daily life

Few technological breakthroughs have had as great an impact on our lives as the computer. It has made some long and complicated tasks quick and easy; it also does many routine work tasks, freeing people to do more important and interesting jobs.

Write an essay of about 200 words about how the computer has had an impact on daily life. You may discuss positive or negative aspects of the computer's influence, or both. Give examples to support your ideas.

In the sample topic above, the subject you're asked to write about is *the computer*. The specific instructions tell you to write about *how the computer has had an impact on daily life*. This is another way of saying the **effects** of the computer on daily life.

The rest of this chapter will help you to understand the specific instructions in different GED essay topics. Several sample topics are given so that you can see how different topics are worded. Of course, not every type of GED essay topic can be covered here. However, the sample topics included will give you a good idea of what to expect when you take the essay portion of the GED Writing Skills Test.

You'll take a closer look at topics that ask you to write about effects. You'll also look at topics that ask you to write about

- the causes of something
- the advantages and disadvantages of something
- the characteristics of something
- your opinion about something

A clear understanding of different kinds of topics will help you to write a good essay.

Effects are outcomes or results. Look again at the sample topic on page 14. It gives you two effects of the computer. According to the topic, the computer has made some long and complicated tasks faster and easier. It also has freed some workers for more interesting jobs.

The diagram below shows the relationship between the computer and these two effects.

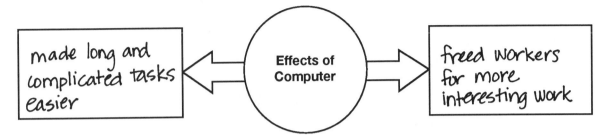

Here are some other ways to ask about effects:

- What **impact** has the computer had on our daily life?
- How has the computer **influenced** our daily life?
- Tell **what happened** when the computer became a part of our daily life.

Which of the following are effects of the computer? Circle any that apply.

(a) fewer people needed to work in some industries

(b) more time needed to complete most routine tasks

(c) more work to complete many complicated tasks

(d) more automation in banks and grocery stores

If you circled (a) and (d), you're correct. These things have happened as a result of the computer. The other choices are not part of the impact of the computer. In other words, they are *not* effects.

> **TEST TIP**
>
> Be on the lookout for key words and phrases, such as *effect* and *result*, in writing topics. Circle them as a reminder of what you are writing about.

What are some other effects of the computer on daily life? List them.

_____

_____

Some GED essay topics ask you to write about **causes**—the reasons why something happens. For example, read the topic below.

Every year, many young people drop out of high school before graduation. They may be bored or frustrated with their education, or they may have obligations that make it hard to stay in school.

Why do so many young people leave school? Write an essay of about 200 words that states your opinion and supports it with specific examples.

In your own words, restate what the specific instructions ask you to write about dropping out.

_____

_____

You're being asked to answer the question *why* people drop out of school. In other words, you must discuss the causes. Here are some other ways to ask about causes:

- **Explain why** people drop out of school.
- **What makes** people drop out of school?
- **What are some reasons** for people dropping out of school?

What are some other ways to talk about causes? List your ideas below.

_____

The diagram sums up the relationship between causes and effects.

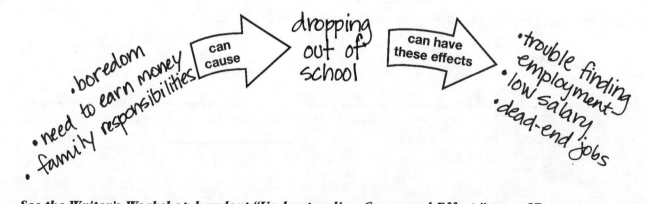

See the Writer's Workshop handout "Understanding Cause and Effect," page 87.

■ **The topics below ask you to write about either effects or causes. For each topic, underline the part of the instructions that indicates cause or effect. Then decide which writer's plan will produce the better essay and circle the letter of the plan.**

---

(1) Many state governments conduct lotteries, a form of legal gambling in which people pay for a ticket and hope that their numbers are selected in a random drawing. Some of the money collected goes to the winners; the rest is used for public needs such as schools and highways. What do you think are the effects of state lotteries on society? Write an essay of about 200 words stating and supporting your opinion.

Writer A: *"I'm going to write about why the state decided to hold lotteries."*

Writer B: *"Lotteries take advantage of poor people, and I'm going to write about this negative effect."*

---

(2) Parents have an effect on their children. Whether it is positive or negative, parental influence is the most powerful external factor in determining a child's personality.

Write an essay of about 200 words explaining one or both of your parents' influences on you as a person. You may discuss positive or negative aspects, or both.

Writer A: *"My plan is to write about what caused my parents to treat me badly and why I resent them for it."*

Writer B: *"I want to write about the fact that I'm a positive thinker because my mother always taught me to see the good side."*

---

(3) It seems that more and more Americans are exercising and watching what they eat. What do you think is causing this "fitness kick"? Write an essay of about 200 words that tells the causes of the "fitness kick" and gives examples.

Writer A: *"I'll write that people are into fitness because they know a lot more about health issues than they used to."*

Writer B: *"I want to write that this fitness kick is making it hard to live as an overweight couch potato."*

Check your answers on page 75-76.

Some GED topics ask you to discuss advantages (pros) and/or disadvantages (cons) in your essay. Below is an example of this type of topic.

While many people consider the daytime to be "normal" working hours, millions of people work at night. Newspaper printers, emergency-room doctors, and truck drivers are just some of the people who may be starting their workday as the rest of us turn off the late show.

Write an essay of about 200 words that discusses the advantages, the disadvantages, or both of working during the night. Use specific examples and reasons in your answer.

The specific instructions in this topic ask you to discuss the **advantages and/or disadvantages** of working during the night. In other words, you must write about the good points and/or bad points.

- Could you write only about the advantages?   yes / no
- Could you write only about the disadvantages?   yes / no
- Could you write about both advantages and disadvantages?   yes / no

The answer to all three questions is yes. The specific instructions give you all three choices.

Make sure that you understand what advantages and disadvantages are. Take a few minutes to jot down some ideas in each of the columns below.

Advantages of Working at Night	Disadvantages of Working at Night

Read the topic at right. Then circle the letter of the instructions that best describe what you are being asked to discuss in your essay.

(a) Discuss the causes of a good friendship.

(b) Discuss the effects of being a good friend.

(c) Discuss the advantages and disadvantages of having a friend.

(d) Discuss the qualities that are important in a friend.

(e) Discuss the good and bad qualities of your best friend.

> Different people look for different qualities in a friend. Some people want friends whose interests are the same as their own. Others look for people who are easy to talk with. Still others look for people whom they admire.
>
> Write an essay of about 200 words describing the characteristics you think are important in a friend. Be specific and give examples showing what you mean.

Did you circle (d)? A topic that asks you to write about **characteristics** is asking you about the qualities, or traits, of someone or something. You don't need to write about *all* the qualities—just some that you think are important.

WRITING YOUR OPINION

Directly or indirectly, all GED essay topics ask you to state your opinion. Your **opinion** is your belief, or point of view, about a subject. There is no such thing as a "right" or "wrong" opinion. The people who evaluate your essay will *not* penalize you if they disagree with the opinion you state. Instead, they'll be looking to see whether you clearly stated and supported your opinion. Here are a few examples of topics that ask you to state your opinion:

- Should the state government run lotteries?
- Do professional athletes make too much money?
- Are people today more self-centered than they were in the past?
- Are prisons effective in America's fight against crime?

Remember: The purpose of your essay on any of these topics is to *state what you think* and then *discuss why* you think that way.

PART ONE

■ **Read each topic. Then decide which writer's plan will produce the best essay and circle that writer's letter.**

(1) Write an essay that discusses the advantages, the disadvantages, or both of working during the night. Use specific examples and reasons in your answer.

> **Writer A:** *"I think I'll write about why a diner needs an all-night cook."*

> **Writer B:** *"Working at night allows you to avoid rush-hour traffic and do errands during the day. I'll write about that."*

> **Writer C:** *"I know a lot of night jobs—my essay will give a list of them."*

(2) Why do so many young people leave school? Write an essay that states your opinion and supports it with specific examples.

> **Writer A:** *"I'll write that the causes of people leaving school are mainly economic."*

> **Writer B:** *"When people leave school, they don't get good jobs, they make less money, and they don't feel good about life. I'll write about these things."*

> **Writer C:** *"My essay will tell why dropping out of school is a lousy idea."*

(3) Write an essay that identifies the qualities you think a good employer has, giving specific examples to back up your ideas.

> **Writer A:** *"I'm going to write about how bad employers make it difficult to get work done."*

> **Writer B:** *"There are many advantages to working for a good employer. My essay will discuss these advantages and give examples."*

> **Writer C:** *"I think good employers are always honest and fair. I'm going to give examples of these qualities and why they're important."*

(4) What do you think is causing American interest in exercise and diet? Write an essay that tells the causes of the "fitness kick" and gives examples.

> **Writer A:** *"The diet craze is causing teenagers to starve themselves. My essay will discuss how harmful these diets can be."*

> **Writer B:** *"My essay will discuss the fact that people are obsessed with how they look and that this is the main reason they are 'fitness-crazy.' "*

> **Writer C:** *"If you exercise and diet wisely, you can dramatically improve your health. This is the main advantage of the fitness craze that I'll discuss in my essay."*

PART TWO

■ **Choose one of the topics from Part One. Jot down some ideas in the space below; then write one or two paragraphs in response to the topic.**

Jot down your ideas here.

Check your answers on page 76.

A good way to ensure that you understand GED essay topics is to write a few of your own. Use two of the general topics listed below to write GED-type essay topics. Copy the form you have seen in all the sample topics in this chapter. Make sure that each of your topics has a background statement and specific instructions that include the 200-word guideline.

You and your partner may write your topics together, or you may write them separately and review each other's work.

General Topics

- reasons why people do not vote
- what happens when people do not vote
- qualities of a good relationship
- whether teachers should be paid more than police officers

GED essay topic 1

Background statement: _____

_____

_____

Specific instructions: _____

_____

GED essay topic 2

Background statement: _____

_____

_____

Specific instructions: _____

_____

THE WRITING PROCESS

☑ PREWRITING

1. Understand the test
2. Analyze the topic
3. Generate ideas and make a plan
   - Brainstorming and clustering
   - Using the idea circle
   - Choosing an angle
   - Finding and writing your main idea
   - Sorting through your ideas
   - Thinking about your writing plan

☐ DRAFTING

4. Write the essay

☐ REVISING

5. Read over and improve the essay
6. Use good test-taking strategies

■ **In the space below, write down everything you think of when you see the word *test*. You can write sentences, short ideas, or just single words. Keep writing whatever pops into your head. Don't worry about making mistakes!**

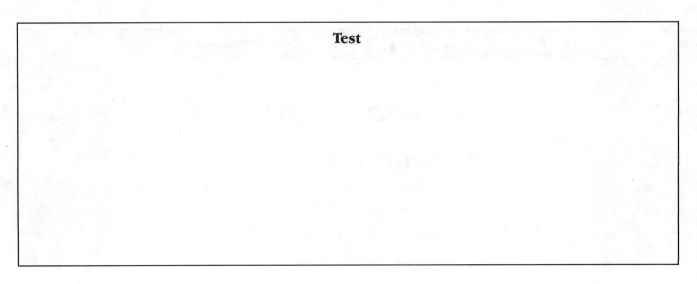

Test

This activity is a kind of **brainstorming**—letting your mind be free and open to all thoughts about a subject. Your brainstorming list may have some ideas in common with another person's. However, it may also contain different ideas, because your thoughts are your own— no one else's.

For example, one writer's list may look like this:

Test

- *grades, score?*
- *challenge and opportunity*
- *GED diploma, good job*

- *GED Writing Skills Test*
- *December 15, 9:00 A.M.*

This writer focuses on one test—when it will be taken, what it represents, what might come of it. Now look at another writer's brainstorming list about the same word:

Test

- *GED writing sample*
- *driver's test*
- *eye test*
- *blood test*

- *test of character*
- *math test*
- *test of strength*

This writer lists different kinds of tests. Did the ideas on your brainstorming list have anything in common with either of the lists above? What aspect of the word *test* did you focus on?

Brainstorming is a terrific warm-up activity to prepare for the GED essay or any other writing task. Brainstorming can help you discover your thoughts before you put them in essay form. Remember: *your ideas are the most important part of your writing*. If you can't get your ideas on paper, your writing won't be effective.

When you're brainstorming

- write down everything that comes to mind
- remember that there are no right or wrong ideas
- don't worry about spelling and grammar

See the Writer's Workshop handout "Freewriting," page 89.

See the Writer's Workshop handout "Freewriting," page 89.

TEST TIP
When you're brainstorming, try not to "censor" your own ideas. It helps to write down *everything* you can think of about a given subject. You may find later that some ideas are better than you thought!

EXERCISE 1

■ **In the spaces provided, brainstorm about the subjects given.**

(1) violence

(2) money

(3) work

Answers will vary.

■ **Look at how one writer brainstormed about the topic on page 2—how the automobile has affected society. How might this technique help you?**

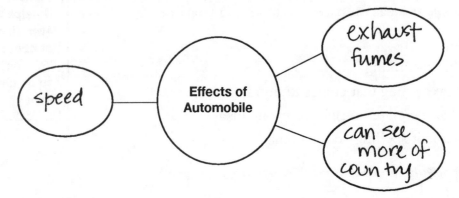

The thinking strategy used above is called **clustering**. To use clustering, you write down and circle your topic in the middle of a piece of paper. Then, as you get ideas about the topic, you write down and circle them, connecting them to related ideas.

For example, the writer above thought of exhaust fumes as an effect of the automobile, so she wrote it down and connected it to the circled topic. Another effect she thought of was speed, and another was the fact that with an automobile, a person can see more of the country. She wrote these ideas down, circled them, and connected them to the main topic they relate to— effects of the automobile.

As she continued clustering, the idea of exhaust fumes made her think of pollution, and pollution made her think of cancer. She added these ideas onto her cluster as shown below. Can you see this writer's thought process in the rest of her clustering?

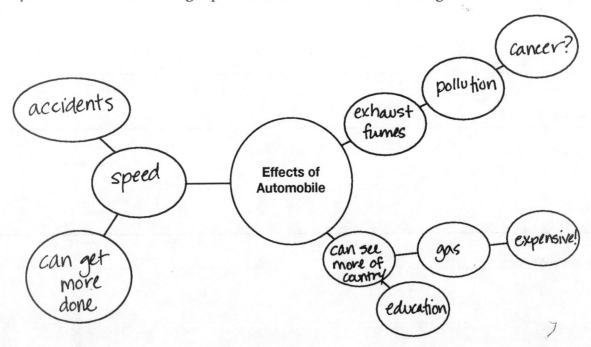

Now use the space below to make your own cluster. The topic is circled. As you think of ideas, connect them to the topic or to other ideas in your cluster to show how they are related. Remember, as with any thinking strategy, there is no right or wrong way to cluster. You're free to cluster in whatever way helps you get ideas on paper.

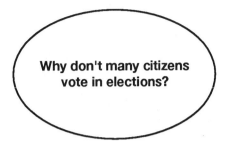

Why don't many citizens vote in elections?

Clustering may work for you, or it may not. This thinking strategy tends to work for people who are visual learners—people who like to see a picture that goes along with words. Practice clustering a few times before you decide whether or not you like it. As with all thinking strategies, the more you use it, the easier it will become.

EXERCISE 2

■ **Try clustering with these topics. *Save your idea clusters.***

(1)

Why do people smoke?

(2)

What are the characteristics of a good friend?

Answers will vary.

■ **Think about the topic below by using this *idea circle*:**

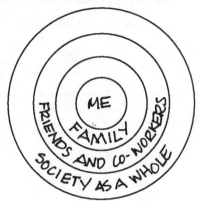

It seems that more and more Americans are exercising and watching what they eat. What do you think is causing this "fitness kick"? Is it primarily concern with health, body image, or something else? Write an essay of about 200 words that tells the causes of the "fitness kick" and gives examples.

Start with the center of the circle. Ask yourself, What does the fitness kick have to do with me, personally? As with brainstorming and clustering, you need to open up your mind and let ideas flow as freely as you can. Begin working through the circle by jotting down ideas in the spaces below.

_____

_____

Now move to the next outer circle. Think about each member of your family. Is one of them fitness crazy? If not, imagine why a family member might be interested in fitness.

_____

_____

The next circle is co-workers and friends. Does someone you work with exercise a lot? What might be his or her reasons? Has a friend ever talked about dieting?

_____

_____

The outermost circle refers to society as a whole. What have you heard about dieting and exercise in the newspaper or on TV?

_____

_____

You may have more ideas about one area than another. That's OK. Remember that the idea circle is just a way to stimulate your thinking and get your mind working in a productive way. There aren't any right or wrong ways to think!

Here's how one writer used the idea circle to generate ideas for the fitness topic.

The fitness craze and me
- *I don't need to lose weight.*
- *I'm not particularly careful about what I eat.*
- *I hate to exercise and almost never do.*

The fitness craze and family members
- *Dianne diets to lose weight to look good.*
- *Dad exercises to keep his heart healthy.*
- *Lou has stopped eating fried food and sweets.*

The fitness craze and my friends
- *Sam says red meat and salt are bad for health.*
- *Sandy wants to look like a model on TV.*
- *Juan works out five days a week.*

The fitness craze in society as a whole
- *There's more information on how to stay healthy and live longer.*
- *New studies show how eating and exercise affect health.*
- *There are lots of fitness magazines nowadays.*

Don't be discouraged if you're still having trouble coming up with ideas. Relax and keep trying. The more practice you get with these thinking strategies, the easier they will become.

■ **Use the idea circle to jot down ideas for the following topics. Answer the questions accompanying the first topic to guide yourself through the thinking process. Then fill in the blanks to complete work on the second topic.** *Save your lists. You'll need them later.*

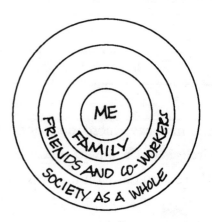

Topic 1

Every year, many young people drop out of high school before graduation. They may be bored or frustrated with their education, or they may have obligations that make it hard to stay in school.

Why do so many young people leave school? Write an essay of about 200 words that states your opinion and supports it with specific examples.

(a) Start with the center circle. Did you drop out of school? Why? If you are in school now, what might cause you to drop out?

_____

_____

(b) Move to the next layer of the circle. Has a family member dropped out of school? What was the reason?

_____

_____

(c) How about friends and co-workers? Have you ever heard any of them discussing dropouts?

_____

_____

(d) Think about society as a whole. What have you heard on television about the dropout rate and why it is so high in this country?

_____

_____

Topic 2

"It's a terrible shame that young people spend so much of their time staring at television. If we unplugged all the television sets, our children would grow up to be healthier, better educated, and more independent."

Do you agree or disagree with this statement? Write an essay of about 200 words presenting your point of view and supporting it with specific examples from your own experience or your observations of others.

Self: _____

_____

Family: _____

_____

Friends/Co-workers: _____

_____

Society: _____

_____

Answers will vary.

If you wrote everything there is to say about a topic, your essay would be hundreds of pages long! To avoid overwriting and to focus your ideas, think about the topic from these four different **angles**, or perspectives:

PERSONAL

ECONOMIC

PHYSICAL

SOCIAL

Look at the following topic to see how this strategy works.

The automobile has been responsible for many changes in the United States. Some of these changes have improved our lives. Some have made life more difficult.

Write an essay of about 200 words describing the effects of the automobile on modern life. You may describe the good effects, the bad effects, or both. Be specific and use examples to support your view.

Instead of just writing down every effect of the automobile you can think of, try organizing your thinking by brainstorming about the angles listed above. Here's how one writer did this:

Personal

- *I can visit the country with a car.*
- *I spend too much money on gas!*

Economic

- *Lots of jobs were created when the car was invented.*
- *Many people spend too much money on cars.*

Physical

- *Riding is easier than walking.*
- *Cars can make people lazy.*

Social

- *Cars make it easier to see friends.*
- *Ambulances save people's lives.*

Remember that it's OK to adapt this or any other thinking technique to suit your needs. For example, when you use the Choose-an-Angle technique, you don't have to brainstorm about all four categories. If you want, just write down ideas for the angles that you have the most ideas about.

EXERCISE 4

■ **For the topic below, use the Choose-an-Angle technique to generate ideas. Write about as many of the four categories as you can.** *Save your idea list. You'll use it later in this chapter.*

More and more homes now are equipped with modern technological conveniences and entertainment devices such as portable phones, big-screen TVs, VCRs, and compact disc players. The result of having these items at home is that people are tending to go out less frequently.

Write an essay of about 200 words that discusses the effects of this "stay-at-home" lifestyle. You may discuss the positive effects, the negative effects, or both.

Personal   **Economic**

Physical   **Social**

Answers will vary.

■ **Read the essay below on the topic** *Why do people smoke?* **What point is the writer trying to make?**

> *People smoke for different reasons. The first reason is that they are addicted—they can't break the habit. The second reason is that they constantly see advertising that tells them smoking is cool.*
>
> *Research has shown that the nicotine in cigarettes is addictive. Everyone needs to understand that quitting smoking is not as easy as just saying you want to. After years and years of smoking two packs a day, a person is going to need serious medical help if he or she wants to stop. Stopping smoking is a major lifestyle change for lots of people.*
>
> *And it sure must be hard to kick the habit when you are always seeing skinny, beautiful women and handsome macho men puffing away. Cigarette advertising should be illegal because it takes advantage of people who are already hurting—smokers. Teenagers are really the targets of this kind of glamorous advertising—they want a cool image so they smoke.*

So far in the writing process, you've analyzed the topic and generated some ideas about it. The next step in the process is to figure out what the **main idea** of your essay will be.

The topic for the essay above asks, *Why do people smoke?* On the line below, write down what this writer thinks the causes are. In other words, write his main idea.

_____

Recall that a main idea should clearly state what the essay will be about. For example, in an essay about the reasons for smoking, the main idea should state why people smoke. The writer above clearly states that people smoke because of their addiction and the advertising they see. The rest of the essay explains this main idea.

TEST TIP

Always state your main idea in the first sentence or in the first paragraph of your essay. Doing this will help you organize your essay.

Now look at the list of ideas below and see if you can decide what the writer's main idea is. The topic is the effects of state-run lotteries.

- *People have fun—they get a chance to be a millionaire.*
- *Everybody benefits somehow.*

- *State services improve with the extra funds.*
- *State needs the money—what's the harm?*

Circle the writer's main idea.

(a) State-run lotteries benefit people in a lot of ways.

(b) There are many pros and cons to state-run lotteries.

(c) State-run lotteries are good because I might win.

Did you circle (a)? If so, you understand what the main idea of an essay should do. The writer's brainstorming list gives examples of the benefits of a lottery. These ideas support the main idea that state-run lotteries benefit people in a lot of ways.

EXERCISE 5

■ **Read each brainstorming list. Then circle the letter of the main idea of the list. The topic is *What are the advantages, disadvantages, or both of living in the city?***

List 1

- *crowded*
- *polluted*

- *too much crime*
- *hurried lifestyle*

- *mean people*
- *hard to make friends*

(a) The disadvantages of city living all relate to expense.

(b) The city is a great place to live because of its rich diversity.

(c) Crowds, crime, and unhappy people are the city's disadvantages.

List 2

- *museums, concerts, restaurants*

- *close to everything*
- *close to work*

- *no need to leave*
- *great public transportation*

(a) The biggest disadvantage to city living is how dirty it is.

(b) The most obvious advantage to city living is convenience.

(c) There are both advantages and disadvantages to city living.

Check your answers on page 76.

■ **Look at the list of ideas that one person wrote down in response to the topic _Why don't more people vote in elections?_ Then, on the lines below, write down the main idea that this writer should use in his essay. Be sure to use a complete sentence.**

- _No good candidates_
- _Don't think it will make a difference_
- _Mistrust of government_
- _Waste of time_

Main Idea: _____

_____

The ideas above show that this writer thinks people do not vote because they don't like the way our government works. They believe voting is a waste of time and effort. Does your main idea statement sound something like this?

Many people don't vote in elections because they don't think our government is effective.

Each of the ideas in the list above helps to support, or prove, this main idea. Think of the main idea as your point of view—the opinion you want readers to understand.

Here's another list of ideas based on the same topic. What is this writer's main idea?

- _People are lazy._
- _Don't realize how important voting is_
- _People don't bother to learn about candidates._
- _Would rather blame country's problems on someone else_

Main Idea: _____

_____

Can you see that these ideas are different from those in the first list? The point that this writer is making might be summed up like this: *Many Americans don't bother to vote because they don't want to take responsibility for their government.*

Writing a main idea statement is an important part of prewriting. It encourages you to think hard about the ideas you have written down. It also tells the reader what to expect in the essay.

The **main idea** of an essay

- tells the writer's opinion about the topic
- says, in brief, what the essay will be about
- gives a focus, or direction, to the essay

TEST TIP

Once you have written down your ideas, use the same scratch paper to *write down your main idea.* This step will help you stay on topic.

EXERCISE 6

PART ONE

■ Use the guidelines above to write main ideas for the lists below. The topic for these writers is *What are the characteristics of a good job?*

(1)
- *high pay*
- *lots of benefits*
- *three weeks' paid vacation*
- *boss who's out a lot*
- *easy work*

Main Idea: _____

_____

(2)
- *easy commute from home*
- *boss who understands working parents*
- *good daycare close by*
- *flexible hours*

Main Idea: _____

_____

PART TWO

■ Go back to the lists of ideas you came up with in Exercises 2, 3, and 4. Choose three of these lists, and write down a main idea for each. Use complete sentences.

Answers will vary.

Once you have written down your thoughts and decided on your main idea, your next step is to decide which of your ideas to include. Look at this list of ideas from a writer responding to the topic *What are the advantages, disadvantages, or both of living where you do?*

Like
- *good landlord*
- *reasonable rent*
- *warm winters*
- *close to shopping*

Don't Like
- *apartment too small*
- *too far from work*
- *loud neighbors*
- *leaky bathroom faucet*

Main Idea: *There are several advantages to my living situation, but there are also some big disadvantages as well.*

As you can see, this writer plans to discuss both the pros and cons of the place where she lives. Her list of ideas helped her come up with a clear main idea. However, she does not have to include *all* the ideas on her list. What might be some reasons for leaving out some of these ideas?

> **TEST TIP**
>
> Did you notice how this writer separated her list into two columns? This is a great strategy for organizing thoughts.

- After looking over her list, the writer may decide that *warm winters* does not really fit in with the other ideas, which all deal with the apartment itself. Even though she does like warm winters, she may decide to leave out that idea.

- As she thinks about her main idea, the writer may realize that a leaky bathroom faucet is not really a big disadvantage. Even though it's something that she doesn't like about her apartment, she may decide to leave it out.

- The more she thinks about her ideas, the more this writer may lean toward concentrating on only two advantages and one disadvantage. She has a lot to say about her landlord and the distance she travels to work. She may concentrate on these ideas.

Of course, there are many ways to use this list of ideas to write an essay. Remember that the list is meant to help you get your ideas organized and ready to put into essay form.

When you have written down your list of ideas, take a few minutes to

- take out any ideas that don't seem to fit
- shorten your list by deciding what's most important
- add ideas that might help support your main idea

See the Writer's Workshop handout "Irrelevant Ideas," page 91.

TEST TIP

Use your idea list as a guide—not a straitjacket. Feel free to change, take out, or add any ideas.

EXERCISE 7

PART ONE

■ Suppose that in response to the topic on the previous page you came up with the idea list below. Using these ideas, write a main idea statement. Work with these ideas as if they were your own. Feel free to make any changes that you like in the list.

Good Things

- *roof over my head*
- *nice neighbors*

Bad Things

- *scary neighborhood*
- *run-down building*
- *more money than I can afford*

Main Idea: _____

_____

PART TWO

■ Using your own lists and main idea statements from Exercise 6, Part Two, on page 37, sort through your ideas and make any changes and additions that might help your essay. *Remember to save your work.*

So far, you've completed these steps in the writing process:

(1) analyzed the topic

(2) written a list of ideas

(3) written a main idea statement

(4) sorted through your list

In short, you have almost finished prewriting, or developing a **writing plan**. By this point in the writing process, you should have a good idea of what your essay is going to say.

To make sure you stay on target, you need to "talk yourself through" your writing plan one last time. Here's an example of how one writer decided to handle her GED writing topic.

In response to the topic *What are the good and/or bad aspects of where you live?* the writer used the PEPS strategy (pages 32–33) to come up with the following ideas:

Personal
- *nice, quiet neighborhood*
- *a little isolated—lonely*

Economic
- *low rent*
- *expensive commute to work*

Physical
- *pretty run-down*
- *needs painting, new floors*

Social
- *too far from my family/friends*

The writer thought about her ideas and decided that most were negative aspects. Although her rent was low and the neighborhood was OK, there was a lot more that she *disliked* about her home than she liked. She wrote the following main idea statement:

> *By having to think about this topic, I must admit that there are a few major disadvantages to living where I do.*

Once she decided on this approach to the topic, the writer sorted through her ideas and circled those that she planned to use in her essay.

Personal
- *nice, quiet neighborhood*
- *a little isolated—lonely*

Physical
- *pretty run-down*
- *needs painting, new floors*

Economic
- *low rent*
- *expensive commute to work*

Social
- *too far from my family/friends*

Here's how this writer "talked herself through" her writing plan:

> *"I'm going to write only about the negative aspects of where I live. From my list, it looks like the two big problems are that I live too far from everything and the apartment is in bad physical shape. I'll write about the distance problem first. Then, I'll describe how run-down the place is—I can give lots of examples of things that need repair."*

Remember that this writer could have chosen a different way to respond to the topic. You will be able to respond to your topic in different ways, too. That's why it's important to talk yourself through your plan. Then you won't be tempted to use ideas that don't belong. In Chapter 4, you'll see problems that occur when a writer doesn't have a clear plan.

> **TEST TIP**
>
> Once you've come up with a writing plan, *stick to it*. Use it as a guide for everything you put into your essay.

EXERCISE 8

■ **In Exercise 7, you sorted your ideas in three of your lists. Now "talk yourself through" a writing plan for one of your lists. Jot down the plan on the lines below.**

_____

_____

_____

_____

_____

_____

_____

_____

Answers will vary.

Have you ever heard the expression "Two heads are better than one"? With a partner, practice using different thinking strategies to generate ideas. You'll be amazed at how many different ideas two people can come up with.

Why do an activity like this when you won't be allowed to work with a partner during the GED test? By practicing with a partner, you can learn by *seeing how other people think*. Perhaps one partner has a strategy that works well for certain topics. The other partner may be able to explain how to use a different strategy. Learning how other writers work is a terrific way to improve your own writing skills.

For each topic below, see how many different ideas you can generate with your partner. Use any of the thinking strategies you learned in this chapter.

Topic 1

Cigarettes cannot be advertised on television, but cigarette advertising is permitted in newspapers and magazines, and cigarette manufacturers regularly sponsor sporting events.

Should cigarette advertising be permitted at all in this country? Write an essay of about 200 words in which you present your opinion and support it with specific reasons and examples.

Topic 2

The crime rate in urban areas in our country keeps going up and up. Everyone from politicians to crime victims to criminals has an opinion about why. Some blame the economy, some blame the collapse of the family, and some blame drugs.

What do you think are the major causes of our high crime rate? Use specific examples to support your opinions.

THE WRITING PROCESS

☑ PREWRITING

1. Understand the test
2. Analyze the topic
3. Generate ideas and make a plan

☑ DRAFTING

4. Write the essay
   - Analyzing the parts of an essay
   - Writing an introduction
   - Putting ideas in paragraphs
   - Using examples
   - Writing a conclusion
   - Avoiding common pitfalls

☐ REVISING

5. Read over and improve the essay
6. Use good test-taking strategies

In the last chapter, you developed a plan for writing. Now that you have a plan, you're ready to start writing your essay. Read the topic below. Then look closely at the essay that follows. Notice the different parts of an effective GED essay.

> Think about how many advertisements you see and hear around you every day. You read and hear claims about all kinds of products and services—from soap to car loans. Ads give information, and they try to persuade us.
>
> Write an essay of about 200 words discussing the effects of advertising on our lives. You may write about the positive effects, the negative, or both. Be specific and be sure to support your point of view.

Main idea statement

Introduction

Advertisements may be annoying, but they actually serve many different purposes, and their overall effect on society is a positive one. First, advertising is a way to get information to people. Second, advertising increases sales, which creates more jobs for people. And lastly, advertising pays for all the great articles we have in print and shows we have on TV.

Body

Maybe we don't always feel like seeing another commercial for laundry detergent. However, commercials also give us information about drug abuse hot lines, charity drives, and products that may be useful if we even knew they existed! Advertising gives us information that we can often use.

Without advertising, there would be fewer jobs. Advertising can keep competing companies in business. By letting the marketplace know the advantages of their products or services, companies can prosper.

Finally, newspapers, magazines, and television networks survive by selling advertising time and space. Without ads, there wouldn't be any of the good network TV shows, newspaper articles, or magazine features that we all enjoy.

Conclusion

Although we may get tired and annoyed by advertising, it is a necessary and useful part of society. And don't forget, no one is forcing us to see it.

Can you see how each idea presented in the introduction is explained and developed in one of the body paragraphs?

Most effective essays have a structure that consists of three major parts:

(1) The **introduction**, which tells what the essay will be about. It gives a preview of what will follow. The introduction includes a main idea statement.

(2) One or more **body paragraphs**, which support the main idea expressed in the introduction. They add details that help the reader understand the main idea.

(3) A **conclusion**, which summarizes what has just been said in the body paragraphs.

> **TEST TIP**
>
> Here's an easy way to remember what to say in each part of an essay.
> **Introduction:** Tell the reader what you're going to write about.
> **Body:** Write about it.
> **Conclusion:** Tell the reader what you just wrote about.

EXERCISE 1

■ **Read the essay below. Underline the main idea statement. Then underline each idea presented in the introduction and draw an arrow from it to the body paragraph that explains it. Last, underline the sentence in the conclusion that sums up the main idea.**

The effects of advertising on our society today are entirely negative. Advertising insults our intelligence and takes up precious time and space. In addition, advertising is ruining the minds of the young children and adolescents who are exposed to it.

Think about how great things would be without all those advertisers telling us which gum to chew and soda to drink. They think that we can't make up our own minds! The time and space advertising consumes could be used for longer shows and better things to read.

Young people are likely to be greatly influenced by what they see and hear. Not knowing any better, kids may believe advertisements that make false claims. Furthermore, alcohol and cigarette advertising can steer kids down the wrong path.

Advertising adds nothing positive to our society. We'd be better off if we took all the money spent on these ridiculous commercials and used it to improve the goods and services being sold.

Check you answers on page 76.

WRITING AN INTRODUCTION

The introductions below were written in response to the advertising topic on page 44. Which is more effective? (circle one)

(a) *Seeing so many advertisements is not good for people. All ads are dumb and repetitive. But you can learn things sometimes from watching commercials, such as where to find a particular product. Fewer ads would be nice, but then TV stations would lose money.*

(b) *The effects of advertising on our society are both positive and negative. First of all, advertising creates jobs by helping to increase sales of goods and services. On the other hand, advertising seems to be turning Americans into materialistic consumers who value possessions over just about everything else.*

Will the writer of the first introduction be discussing positive effects, negative effects, or both? You can't tell, can you? In her short paragraph, she starts out by saying that seeing advertisements is not good. But then she contradicts this statement with an example of a positive effect of advertisements. Finally, she includes an unrelated idea about television stations losing money. It's unclear what her essay will be about.

The writer of the second introduction clearly tells what the essay will be about. The first sentence—his main idea statement—tells you that he'll discuss both positive and negative effects. In addition, the introduction tells you that two ideas will be discussed in the essay—advertising creates jobs, but advertising also makes people more materialistic. In short, this introduction gives a good overview of what the essay will be about.

> **TEST TIP**
>
> A good introduction
> - clearly states the main idea of the essay
> - gives a preview of the essay's content
> - is usually three or four sentences long

A clear main idea statement is an excellent way to begin an introduction. Look at how one writer turned her list of ideas and main idea statement about advertising into an introduction.

Positive Effects of Advertising
- *entertaining*
- *informative*

Negative Effects
- *interruptions can be irritating*

Main Idea Statement: *Although the interruptions can sometimes be irritating, the positive effects of advertising outweigh the negative.*

Introduction: *Although the interruptions can sometimes be irritating, the positive effects of advertising outweigh the negative. Many commercials are really entertaining and make me laugh. Others provide useful information that is not found elsewhere.*

Can you see how the writer used her main idea statement and some of her supporting ideas to tell what the essay will be about? In the main idea statement, she tells readers that she believes the positive effects of advertising outweigh the negative. Then she gives a preview of the content of the body by mentioning two positive effects of advertising—it can be entertaining, and it can be informative. Notice that the writer doesn't use the introduction to explain and develop the two positive effects of advertising. She knows that the place to develop these ideas is the body of the essay.

See the Writer's Workshop handout "Answering the Topic Question," page 93.

EXERCISE 2

■ **Go back to your revised lists and main idea statements from Chapter 3, Exercise 7, Part Two, page 39. Write an introduction for each main idea. Each introduction should**
- **clearly state your main idea**
- **give a preview of what will follow in the essay**
- **be three or four sentences long**

Answers will vary.

Once your introduction is finished, write the body paragraphs of your essay by using the ideas that you generated earlier. Remember that the body paragraphs should explain, or offer support for, the main idea you stated in the first paragraph. See how the body paragraphs below support the main idea statement.

Main Idea Statement: *Although the interruptions can sometimes be irritating, the positive effects of advertising outweigh the negative.*

Positive Effects of Advertising
- *entertaining*
- *informative*

Although many ads seem stupid, there really is entertainment value in a lot of advertising. For example, the new cola ads are fun to watch, and the music is great. There are lots of commercials like this one that make people laugh or smile.

Advertising also serves the purpose of informing people about different products and services. People can learn about Save the Children and other worthy organizations that need our money. Also, we can be informed of big sales at different stores, which can help us save money.

Notice how this writer took each of the positive effects of advertising and developed it in its own paragraph to support the main idea statement. She added examples to help explain each idea. You'll spend some time working with details and examples later in this chapter. For now, look at another example of putting ideas into paragraphs. The sample introduction and body on the next page are based on the topic below.

The crime rate in urban areas in our country keeps going up. Everyone from politicians to criminals has an opinion on what the causes are. What do you think are the major causes of our high crime rate? Write an essay of about 200 words stating your opinion. Be sure to use specific examples to support your ideas.

Here's how one writer used clustering and then put his ideas into paragraphs.

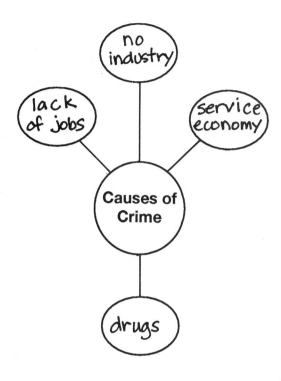

Writing Plan
I'll write about crime being caused by no jobs in the city and the drug problem.

The crime rate in this country is getting higher and higher because our cities are being ignored. First of all, there are no jobs for city residents. Industry has left these people behind. Secondly, drugs have become a way of life for young people, and no one has a good plan to tackle the problem. Because drug abuse is seen as a city problem, the problem is ignored.

Since there are few jobs in the city, kids turn to robbery and mugging to get money to survive. It becomes an accepted way to live—if everyone else is doing it, it must be okay. If there were good jobs available, people would be busy working and earning money, and the crime rate would go down.

Drugs are also a related cause for the crime rate. Everybody in the city knows that the easiest way to earn a lot of money is to deal drugs. Then, the more people who are hooked on drugs, the more people who need money to buy drugs and the more people who commit crime to get drugs. To make matters worse, drugs make people act crazy and more willing to commit ugly crimes like murder.

Take some time to investigate how this writer put his ideas in paragraph form. Notice how he expanded some ideas on his list. Also notice that he did not include all ideas from his cluster. He used only the ideas that fit into his writing plan.

EXERCISE 3

■ **Go back to your revised lists and main idea statements from Chapter 3, Exercise 7, Part Two, on page 39. You have already written an introduction for each. Now choose one introduction and write the body paragraphs for this essay. Remember to follow your writing plan and use only the ideas that support your main idea.**

Answers will vary.

USING SPECIFIC EXAMPLES

The following paragraphs are about the crime topic on page 48. In which paragraph is the main idea easier to understand? (circle one)

(a) *One reason for the high crime rate in America is that family values are no longer a part of society. More and more kids are being born to single mothers who cannot afford to take care of them alone. Parents are not teaching children the difference between right and wrong. Spouse and child abuse is everywhere. The family should be a higher priority.*

(b) *Who is responsible for the high crime rate in the United States? People are. We are the only ones who can tackle the problem, and it is a big problem. Unless people get together and do something fast, the crime rate will only get higher.*

You may sense that paragraph (a) is the more effective of the two. Can you tell why? The writer says that the lack of family values is one reason for the high crime rate. But he doesn't just *tell* us that. He *shows* us what he means. He gives **examples**, or specific instances, of a lack of family values in our country.

The writer of paragraph (b) tells us that people are the cause of the high crime rate, but he doesn't show us how or why people are the cause. We are left wondering, because he doesn't give us examples to support his main idea.

SHOW WHAT YOU MEAN

Examples can come from a lot of different sources. They can come from your own experience, from things you have read in the newspaper and heard about on TV, or from talking with and observing other people.

Read the following statement ...ken from a GED essay. Try adding an example to really *show* what the writer means. Answer the questions to get yourself thinking.

- *People should do more volunteer work in the community.*

   For example, _____

- What kind of volunteer work?
- Why would doing volunteer work be good for the volunteer or the community?
- What volunteer work do you—or people whom you know—do?

Compare your examples to the example below. Notice how specific examples make the sentences come alive.

- *People should do more volunteer work in the community. <u>For example, volunteering as a reader to the blind or a babysitter at a homeless shelter can be rewarding to everyone involved.</u>*

- *People should do more volunteer work in the community. <u>For example, my mother's volunteer work at the hospital cheers up the patients, helps out the overworked staff, and even makes my mom feel good about herself.</u>*

EXERCISE 4

■ **Add examples to the statements below. Answer the questions to think of ideas.**

(1) *One advantage to having a steady job is being able to plan how you will spend your money.*

    For example, _____

_____

_____

      • Why might someone want to plan how to spend money?
      • Have you ever planned how you'll spend your money?
      • What might happen if you didn't have a spending plan?

(2) *We are lucky to be citizens of a free country.* _____

_____

_____

      • What might happen if we didn't live in a free country?
      • What specific advantages are there to being free?
      • How might you be different if you lived elsewhere?

Check your answers on page 77.

See the Writer's Workshop handout "Show, Don't Tell," page 95.

WRITING A CONCLUSION

Go back and read the essay introduction and body on page 49, which were written in response to the topic about crime in our country. Which of the following paragraphs would make a better conclusion for this essay? (circle one)

(a) *There are so many different causes for the crime rate. Our laws and court system don't work, and criminals go free to commit more crime. There are no jobs to help people lead productive lives. And most importantly, television violence tells young people that it's okay to steal and kill.*

(b) *If the United States really wants to reduce its crime rate, it will have to get more industry in the inner city so that people can work and lead productive lives. It will also have to commit itself to a war on drugs that will once and for all get rid of the addicts who are committing the crimes.*

The first paragraph might be an effective conclusion to an essay about the crime rate, but it is *not* a good conclusion for the essay on page 49. The ideas mentioned in this paragraph—laws and courts and television violence—aren't discussed in the essay. The second paragraph *is* an effective conclusion for the essay. It gives a summary of what was discussed in the introduction and body paragraphs on page 49.

Read the following essay. On the lines provided on the next page, write a short conclusion that summarizes the writer's main idea.

> *Our country's crime rate is a disgrace. Instead of working hard to improve the lives of poor people so that they do not need to commit crime, what does the government do? It builds more and more jails and makes it harder and harder for people to lead crime-free lives. The crime rate is getting higher because the government isn't responding to the real problem: poverty.*
>
> *Putting a person in jail for a year does absolutely nothing to encourage him or her to stop committing crime. While in jail, the criminal can't look for a job, can't take care of a family, can't go to school, can't work on getting his or her life in order.*
>
> *People commit crimes because they are desperate. They need food, clothing, somewhere to live, and some quality in their lives. Because there are no jobs to pull people out of poverty, they have to resort to stealing and worse in order to get by.*

Conclusion: _____

_____

_____

_____

_____

Which of the following ideas did you mention in your conclusion? Put a check mark next to those that you included.

☐ (a) Poverty causes crime.

☐ (b) Not having enough jails causes crime.

☐ (c) The government isn't treating the right problem.

☐ (d) Putting people in jail won't reduce the crime rate.

☐ (e) Putting people in jail might increase the crime rate.

Any of the ideas listed above except (b)—*not having enough jails causes crime*—belong in a conclusion for this essay. Ideas (a), (c), (d), and (e) are all supported by the introductory and body paragraphs.

> **TEST TIP**
>
> A good conclusion sums up what was said in the introduction and the body of the essay.

EXERCISE 5

■ **Write a conclusion for the essay you wrote for Exercise 3, page 49, in this chapter. Remember to summarize the main idea.**

Answers will vary.

As you work on putting your ideas into paragraphs, try to avoid pitfalls that can make your writing less effective. Here are some guidelines.

(1) Stay on topic. All ideas should support your main idea.

At what point in the following essay does the writer go off topic?

The most important issue facing the world today is the environment. If we do not work together to solve the problems of pollution, global warming, landfills, etc., we will have no world left to protect.

Why worry about war when we are already in the process of killing ourselves with polluted water and air? Unless we start forcing industry to clean up its wastes, we won't have an earth to take care of.

The problem of war is very real, especially since more and more countries are able to develop dangerous weapons. When will people realize that we all share this planet and we need to take care of it?

The writer begins by stating that the environment is the most important issue, but in the third paragraph, she strays from this topic onto the topic of war. The paragraph does not stay **on topic** because it does not support the main idea statement.

(2) Do not repeat yourself.

What ideas are repeated unnecessarily in this essay?

There are many advantages to getting a good education. Knowledge helps you make important decisions throughout your life, and it enables you to understand the world around you. And a better education means a better job, which means more money.

If you graduate from high school, you can make more money than if you didn't. And if you go on to more schooling, you can make even more money. If you graduate from college, you can make a lot more money. And the more years you go to school, the more money you will earn. More school means more and more money.

An education also means knowledge, and knowledge helps you survive in this complex world. Whom should you vote for for president? How should I raise my children? What makes people act the way they do? These questions are easier to answer if you've learned something in school.

Did you find that the second paragraph repeats the same idea over and over? This writer would have been better off if he had included examples of how education relates to salary, instead of repeating himself.

(3) Use a lot of details and examples. Avoid generalizing.

Read this paragraph. Do you have questions about the writer's point of view?

Children should not watch a lot of television. It is not good for them to see the kinds of things that are on. For one thing, there is too much violence. There is also too much sex and bad language.

The writer uses very general statements to make her point. Details, reasons, and examples are needed to support these ideas.

EXERCISE 6

■ **Improve the paragraph by filling in specific details. Answer the questions to decide which details to use.**

Children should not watch a lot of television. It is not good for them to see the kinds of things that are on. (Why?) _____ _____

For one thing, there is too much violence. (What is an example?) _____

_____

_____

There is also too much sex and bad language. (What is an example?) _____

_____

Check your answers on page 77.

In this chapter, you've written a complete essay. Now it's time to let someone else read it to give you feedback on how well you got your ideas across.

Exchange essays with a partner. As you read your partner's essay, answer each question on the following checklist. Remember to use the guidelines on the handout "Giving Constructive Criticism," page 85, to make comments and suggestions about each other's work.

Checklist

Yes	No	
☐	☐	Does the introduction include a clear main idea statement?
☐	☐	Does the introduction give a true preview of what comes after it?
☐	☐	Does the essay include specific details and examples that "show" rather than "tell"?
☐	☐	Does the writer stay on topic throughout the essay?
☐	☐	Is there any unnecessary repetition of ideas in the essay?
☐	☐	Are there any ideas that aren't clear?
☐	☐	Is the writer able to avoid generalizations?
☐	☐	Is the conclusion a good summary of what was discussed in the essay?

THE WRITING PROCESS

☑ PREWRITING

1. Understand the test
2. Analyze the topic
3. Generate ideas and make a plan

☑ DRAFTING

4. Write the essay

☑ REVISING

5. Read over and improve the essay
   - Understanding the revision process
   - Using a checklist
   - Revising during the test
   - Analyzing your own writing
6. Use good test-taking strategies

Once you've finished writing your GED essay, take some time to read it over. Make sure you've said what you want to say. This will help you **revise** your essay—in other words, make changes that improve it. **Read the paragraph below and think about how the writer might revise it.**

Poor education is the major problem faceing our country today. Schools are just not teaching the skills that our kids need. They're are high school graduates who cannot read or write. Just imagine what our workplace will be like in a few years. When current students are ready for jobs. Something needs to be done about the quality of our schools before it is too late.

When you revise a GED essay, you need to think about two aspects of revision:
- adding or taking out ideas to make your writing clearer to the reader
- fixing mistakes in grammar and spelling (also known as **editing**)

Would you add or take out any ideas from the paragraph above? What mistakes did you find? How would you fix them? Write down what you would change in this paragraph to make the ideas clearer to the reader.

_____

_____

You may have thought about adding a sentence or changing one a bit. In addition, you probably found some spelling and grammar mistakes. In this chapter, you'll learn ways to improve this paragraph and your own writing. For now, look at the next page to see how the paragraph was revised by its writer. Compare these revisions to the ideas you wrote down on the lines above. Would your revisions be the same as the writer's?

> ### TEST TIP
>
> Remember that it's OK to cross out or add ideas right on your GED essay. There's no need to recopy the whole essay if you've made some changes.

Poor education is the major problem ~~faceing~~ facing *our country today. Schools are just not teaching* | For example, why are sixth-graders learning about drugs instead of math and history?

the skills that our kids need. ∧(There) ~~They're~~ *are high school graduates who cannot read or write. Just*

imagine what our workplace will be like in a few years, ~~when~~ when *current students are ready for*

jobs. Something needs to be done about the quality of our schools before it is too late.

EXERCISE 1

■ **Make any revisions you think would improve the quality of each paragraph below. Use your own ideas of what effective writing is, keeping in mind what you have learned so far in this book. (Make your changes right on the paragraphs themselves.)**

(1) *The ongoing wars throughout the world today are the biggest problem The United states faces. Even though they are taking place thousands of miles away, they affect us indirectly. So much of our budget goes toward Economic assistance to struggling nations we even send our own young soldiers to fight in others' battles. And protect weaker countries. Soldiers make a lot of money these days. If the U.S. did not have to involve itself in the wars of others, it could concentrate on its own problems. Their are plenty.*

(2) *Fast-food restaurants are all over the place today because people just don't care anymore. They don't care about eating helthy foods, they don't care about wasteing money, and they don't care about hard work. For example, people say, "Why spend the day making homemade soup. When I can get the same stuff at the drive-thru for $.99?" People don't realize that they are losing a lot—money, helth, and personal satisfaction—every time they order up Fast Food. Its alot cheaper to make soup than to buy it. The satisfaction of doing a job well is tremendous.*

(3) *Living out in the country has many advantages. The piece of mind you get from nowing you are safe can add years to you're life. Can you ever be truly relaxed in the crime-ridden city? No. In addition, country life is cheaper than city life you don't have to spend a lot of money on taxes or rent and theres not an awful lot you can spend your money on. No movies, expensive restaurants, shows, and concerts. But you can spend a lot to get anywhere out of the country! And of course, the beauty of nature is so much more abundant in the country.*

Check your answers on page 77.

REVISING CHECKLIST

Because of the time limit on the essay portion of the GED Writing Skills Test, you may not have all the time you'd like to revise your writing. Try to make those changes and corrections that you feel are most important in getting your point across.

The checklist below gives some guidelines for revising your GED essay. It contains questions you should answer as you revise your writing. When you revise, read over your essay twice. It's a good idea to look at your *ideas* first, then the words.

Revising the Ideas

Yes	No	
☐	☐	Does my introduction let the reader know what my essay will be about?
☐	☐	Is my main idea clear?
☐	☐	Do the ideas in each paragraph support the main idea?
☐	☐	Should I include more examples to make my writing clearer?
☐	☐	Does my conclusion sum up what the essay was about?

Editing the Words

Yes	No	
☐	☐	Do I have any **run-ons**, that is, run-together sentences? *(See the Writer's Workshop handouts "Pulling Apart Run-On Sentences," page 97, and "Adding Connecting Words to Run-On Sentences," page 99.)*
☐	☐	Are there any **sentence fragments**, that is, incomplete sentences? *(See the Writer's Workshop handouts "Sentence Fragments," page 101, and "Sentence Fragments in a Paragraph," page 103.)*
☐	☐	Are all words spelled correctly—particularly those that I often misspell? *(See the Writer's Workshop handout "Commonly Misspelled Words," page 105.)*
☐	☐	Did I use capital letters correctly?

■ Read the essay topic below. Then read the essay based on the topic. Using the checklist, make any revisions you think will improve the writing. (Make changes right on this page.) As you complete each revision item on the list, put a check mark in the box. Remember to read the essay twice—once for the ideas, once for correct wording.

When looking for a place to live, people usually have certain characteristics in mind—qualities that they think are important in a house or a neighborhood. Someone might value lots of open space, while another might value good schools.

Write an essay of about 200 words that identifies what you think are the most important characteristics in a home or neighborhood. Be specific and be sure to give reasons for your point of view.

The most important characteristic of a place to live is your neighbors. Without good neighbors, your life can be really bad. Disagreeable neighbors can make your whole life miserable, so that you can't even function each day, a good neighbor can be a terrific plus.

No matter where you live, you have neighbors. If you're neighbor doesn't like you, he can do a lot of harm. For example, if you don't have a good relationship. Your neighbor can turn his stereo up full blast on a Sunday morning—even if he knows its your only day off. Or if you have a lousy neighbor, he might complain to the landlord every time your kids run down the hall. You have enough to worry about at work, with your own family, and in your own situation without dealing with these aggravations.

On the flip side of the coin, a good neighbor can really make your life happier. Have you ever forgotten your key and been relieved to remember that your neighbor keeps a spare for you?

Besides good schools and a beautiful house, good neighbors are the most important thing to have.

Answers will vary.

Below is a sample of how the essay from Exercise 2 might look after it's been revised during the GED test. Compare it to your own work on page 61. When you were revising, did you look for ways to improve both the ideas and the wording of the ideas? Are your revisions similar to those below?

This sentence is crossed out because it says the same thing as the sentence after it.

The most important characteristic of a place to live is your neighbors. ~~Without good neighbors, your life can be really bad.~~ Disagreeable neighbors can make your whole life miserable, so that you can't even function each day, A good neighbor can be a terrific plus.

run-on sentence

No matter where you live, you have neighbors. If **Your** *~~you're~~ neighbor ~~dosn't~~* **doesn't** *like you, he can do a lot of harm. For example, if you don't have a good relationship, ~~Your~~* **your** *neighbor can turn his stereo up full blast on a Sunday morning—even if he knows ~~its~~* **it's** *your only day off. Or if you have a lousy neighbor, he might complain to the landlord every time your kids run down the hall. You have enough to worry about at work, with your own family, and in your own situation without dealing with these aggravations.*

sentence fragment

On the flip side of the coin, a good neighbor can really make your life happier. Have you ever forgotten your key and been relieved to remember that your neighbor keeps a spare for you? <u>*Or how about a neighbor who's easy to talk to and who agrees with you on just about everything?*</u> *An agreeable neighbor is a great thing!*

This paragraph needed another example, so the writer added one.

~~Besides good schools and a beautiful house, good neighbors are the most important thing to have.~~ Neighbors are important. They can make your life miserable, or they can make your life a lot easier.

This conclusion doesn't summarize the essay, so the writer revised it.

As you can see, crossing out and adding ideas is perfectly acceptable on the GED essay test. But be sure to make your revisions neatly, like the revisions on the essay above, so that your essay is easy to read.

Here are some hints that will be useful as you revise during the GED test:

- To cross something out, draw a single line through the words. Be sure the surrounding words are still readable.

  ☐ *Time is one more ~~additional~~ advantage of getting older.*

- If you want to add something that will not fit neatly within the paragraph, write it in the margin, and draw an arrow to where the words or sentence should go.

  ☐ **(See the essay on page 59.)**

- A **caret** (∧) is a mark that means "insert here." In the sentence below, the caret means "Put a period here."

  ☐ *People grow older* ^They *~~they~~ tend to be set in their ways.*

EXERCISE 3

■ **Identify and explain each change the writer made in the following paragraphs.**

>   The ^a Automobile has had an incredible impact on how people live their lives, but the impact has not been all positive. There would be much less pollution if we didn't have any cars. Our cities would be easier to get around in if there were ~~was~~ no cars.
>
>   Cars account for a large part of pollution today. The number of cars on the highway today is very high. Each year the situation—and the air—worsens. Have you ever seen the highways around L.A. at rush hour?
>
>   If there were no automobiles, ^People ~~People~~ would have to rely on other forms of transportation. This would make the cities less congested and more people-friendly. ~~Cars are great because they get you where you're going fast~~!
>
>   The automobile of course has had many positive effects. But if we ignore the negative effects, we are not hearing ~~being~~ the whole story.

Check your answers on page 77.

KNOW YOUR WRITING

Which of the following problems do you think you have most often when you write? (circle all that apply)

(a) writing sentence fragments

(b) misspelling words that sound alike

(c) not including enough specific details and examples

(d) including ideas that don't support the main idea

(e) writing run-on sentences

It may surprise you to learn that writers tend to make the same mistakes again and again. One writer may have a problem using commas correctly, while another may make general statements without supporting them with examples. These writing weaknesses pop up regularly in their work. This is especially true when the writers work within time limits—as you'll be when you take the GED Writing Skills Test.

An excellent strategy in preparing for the GED essay is to become familiar with your own writing weaknesses. If you know what mistakes you usually make, you'll know to watch out for them when you revise your GED essay. For example, if you know that you often write run-on sentences when you're in a hurry, it would be well worth your time to check carefully for these errors. On the other hand, if you know you're an excellent speller and you didn't have trouble with any of the words in your essay, you shouldn't spend a lot of time checking your spelling.

> **TEST TIP**
>
> When you write your GED essay, leave a wide margin on both sides of the page. That way, you'll have plenty of room to revise.

How do you find out your writing weaknesses? Chances are good that you already have some idea of the things that are difficult for you. In addition, the next exercise will help.

Collect as many pieces of your own writing as you can. You can use all the writing exercises you've done in this book, any other school writing you've done, and even notes and letters to friends. **Using the Revising Checklist on page 60 as a starting point, identify any errors you've made in your writing.** You may use the chart below to record your findings, or you may use a technique of your own. Work with a partner if you like. **When you're finished, jot down a revision strategy that you can use during the GED test. List the kinds of errors you'll look for when you revise your GED essay.**

Words You Often Misspell (List them.)	Run-On Sentences	Sentence Fragments	Irrelevant Ideas	Not Enough Specific Details and Examples	Ineffective Introduction
Ineffective Conclusion	Incorrect Use of Capital Letters	Incorrect Verb Form	Other	Other	Other

REVISING STRATEGY

First, I'll look for _____

_____

Then, I'll look for _____

_____

Finally, I'll look for _____

_____

Answers will vary.

In the "Practice with a Partner" on page 56, you received some valuable feedback on the essay you wrote in Chapter 4. Using this information, as well as what you've learned in this chapter, revise your essay. Use the Revising Checklist on page 60 and the "Giving Constructive Criticism" handout on page 85 to direct your work. Also, pay particular attention to any weaknesses that you discovered in your writing while working through this chapter. If you completed the Revising Strategy on the previous page, use your list to look over your essay.

When you're finished marking up your essay, rewrite it below. Be sure to include all your revisions. Compare your essay with the first draft you wrote on page 53. Ask your partner to reread the newly improved essay and to make further suggestions or comments. (Remember: It will *not* be necessary to rewrite your whole essay when you're revising during the GED test. It will be OK to cross out or add ideas as long as your corrections are neat and easy to read.)

THE WRITING PROCESS

☑ PREWRITING

1. Understand the test
2. Analyze the topic
3. Generate ideas and make a plan

☑ DRAFTING

4. Write the essay

☑ REVISING

5. Read over and improve the essay
6. Use good test-taking strategies
   - Using your time wisely
   - Creating your writing strategy

USING TIME WISELY

Which of the following statements is true about the essay portion of the GED Writing Skills Test? (circle one)

(a) You should write as fast as you can because there is a time limit.

(b) You are given 45 minutes to complete your essay, which is plenty of time to plan, write, and revise.

In this book, you've had lots of practice writing an essay. You've learned a process that will help you succeed in writing about the topic effectively. The only thing you have left to do as you prepare for the GED test is to *think about how to use the 45 minutes you are given.*

As you may already know, 45 minutes is plenty of time to plan, write, and revise a GED essay—*if you use the time wisely.* Remember that the people who will score your essay are not looking for perfect writing. They know that your essay is actually just a first draft, written during a test.

Below you will find some general guidelines as to how you might divide up your time. Later in the chapter, you'll have a chance to modify these guidelines to better fit your own strengths and weaknesses as a writer.

> **TEST TIP**
>
> No matter how you decide to use your 45 minutes, be sure you spend at least some time at each stage of the writing process— planning, drafting, and revising.

> **Planning**   5-15 minutes
> **Drafting**   20-30 minutes
> **Revising**   5-10 minutes

EXERCISE 1

■ **Take 45 minutes to write an essay in response to the topic on the next page. As you complete each step of the writing process, glance at a watch or clock and jot down on the chart how much time you spent on each step. This will help you determine your working pattern.**

"Being unmarried is the best lifestyle of all. As a single person, you can do whatever you want, whenever you want. When you want companionship, you can seek it out. But when you don't want it, you have no responsibilities or obligations to anyone. Being single is total freedom, and that's what life is all about."

Do you agree or disagree with this statement? Write an essay of about 200 words that states your opinion and gives reasons to support it. Be specific and give examples.

Planning	——	**minutes**
Drafting	——	**minutes**
Revising	——	**minutes**

_____

_____

_____

_____

_____

_____

_____

_____

_____

Answers will vary.

Which of the following statements is true about the essay portion of the GED Writing Skills Test? (circle one)

(a) There is one correct method for writing the essay, and all writers should follow it.

(b) There are many methods for writing an effective GED essay; you should use those methods that work for you.

When you write your actual GED essay, use the methods that have worked for you in the past. The methods that have worked for you in this book also will work during the test.

What will happen during the test? After you open your test booklet and read the essay topic, you'll begin your work. As you proceed, you'll have some choices to make. You'll need to answer the following questions:

- What method will you use to generate ideas? Brainstorming? Clustering? The idea circle? Choosing an angle?
- How much time will you spend planning? How much time writing?
- What writing weaknesses should you be on the lookout for?

Although you cannot be completely sure of the answers to these questions until you actually see your topic, it's a good idea to go into the test with a **test-taking strategy**—a group of methods that you know have worked for you in the past. Of course, you may decide to make some changes in your strategy when you're actually taking the test. It's OK if you need to adapt your strategy to do your best.

On the next page is an example of one student's test-taking strategy. Read through it and then think about how yours might be different.

My Test-Taking Strategy

Prewriting

☐ *I'll try to understand the test by carefully reading the topic.*

☐ *I'll analyze the topic by reading the background statement and specific instructions.*

☐ *I'll generate ideas by using the idea circle. If this doesn't seem to be working, I'll try clustering. I'll try not to spend more than 10 minutes thinking up ideas.*

Drafting

☐ *Once I have enough ideas, I'll write. I'll write for no more than 20 minutes.*

Revising

☐ *I'll read over my essay. I'll make sure I've included enough examples; then I'll make sure my verbs are in the right form.*

Remember that this is just one writer's strategy. Yours will almost certainly be different. The following exercise will help you develop your own writing plan.

EXERCISE 2

■ **Fill in the blanks below. Use the work you have done throughout this book to determine the best strategy.**

My Test-Taking Strategy

Prewriting

☐ *I'll try to understand the test by carefully reading the topic.*

☐ *I'll analyze the topic by reading the background statement and specific instructions.*

☐ *I'll generate ideas by using _____.*

   If this doesn't seem to be working, I'll try _____.

   I'll try not to spend more than _____ thinking up ideas.

Drafting

☐ *Once I have enough ideas, I'll write. I'll write for no more than ___ minutes.*

Revising

☐ *I'll read over my essay. I'll make sure I've _____; then I'll make sure _____.*

Answers will vary.

If you've completed the exercises in this book, you've come a long way toward preparing for the essay portion of the GED Writing Skills Test. Nevertheless, you may still have some questions about what you should do during the test. Here are answers to questions often asked by people preparing for the GED.

- **What if I read the topic and don't know anything about it?**

  Relax. If your mind draws a blank, it just means you're anxious about taking the test. Remember that you have methods for generating ideas. Start with the method you chose for your test-taking strategy. If you're still having trouble, try another of the methods you learned in this book—brainstorming, clustering, using the idea circle, or choosing an angle. Ideas will come if you relax and remember that you *are* prepared.

- **What if I want to start writing my essay right away? I'm afraid to spend time planning—I won't have enough time to write!**

  Again, relax. The better your planning, the easier your essay will be to write. Keep reminding yourself that 45 minutes is plenty of time in which to plan, write, and revise.

- **What if I run out of time before I can revise?**

  This probably won't happen to you after all the practice this book has given you in planning. But if it does, choose *one* weakness you know you have as a writer, and look over your essay for that one error. And remember—nobody is expected to write a perfect essay.

- **What if I answer in the wrong way? What if the readers don't like what I say?**

  There is no "right" way to respond to any topic. Your writing will be judged on how well you get across your point of view—regardless of whether the readers agree with you. If you follow the guidelines in this book and express an opinion clearly, giving lots of examples, you'll do just fine.

- **What if the readers just pay attention to my spelling mistakes?**

  This won't happen. GED essay readers are trained to pay close attention to organization, support, and correct use of the English language. Look again at the scoring guide on page 83 for more information.

As a final practice for the GED, try writing under conditions similar to those of the test. By following the steps below, your partner can help.

- Use your test-taking strategy and the timing guidelines you determined in Exercise 1 to respond to the topic below.

- Have your partner sit near a watch or clock. As you complete each step of the writing process, signal to your partner. In the chart below, he or she should jot down the time that's passed.

- When you're finished writing, ask your partner to jot down the total time you took to complete the essay.

- After both partners have completed the exercise, discuss with each other how you might use your time differently when you take the GED test. Should you spend more time planning and less writing? Did you have enough time to revise the way you'd like to? Do you want to change your personal writing plan before you take the test?

The legal drinking age in the United States varies from 16 to 21. Some states allow teenagers to buy and consume alcohol, while other states have decided that a person should be an adult to hold this right.

At what age do you think it is appropriate for people to be allowed to consume alcohol? In an essay of about 200 words, state your opinion and give reasons to support it. Be sure to give plenty of examples.

Chart

Time writing began _____
Planning _____ minutes
Drafting _____ minutes
Revising _____ minutes
Time writing completed _____

The directions below are from the essay portion of an actual GED Writing Skills Test. Practice for the test by following the directions. (For this Post-Test, write on your own notebook paper.) When you're finished, you or a partner should evaluate your essay using the scoring guide on page 83.

This part of the Writing Skills Test is intended to determine how well you write. You are asked to write an essay that explains something or presents an opinion on an issue. In preparing your essay, you should take the following steps:

(1) Read carefully the directions and the essay topic given below.

(2) Plan your essay carefully before you write.

(3) Use scratch paper to make any notes.

(4) Write your essay on the lined pages of the separate answer sheet.

(5) Read carefully what you have written and make any changes that will improve your essay.

(6) Check your paragraphs, sentence structure, spelling, punctuation, capitalization, and usage, and make any necessary corrections.

You will have 45 minutes to write on the topic below. Write legibly and use a ballpoint pen so that the evaluators will be able to read your writing.

Write your essay on the lined pages of the separate answer sheet. The notes you make on scratch paper will not be scored.

Your essay will be scored by at least two trained evaluators who will judge it according to its <u>overall effectiveness</u>. They will judge how clearly you make the main point of your composition, how thoroughly you support your ideas, and how clearly and correctly you write throughout the essay.

Topic

"Cheaters never win." Do you agree or disagree with this statement? Write an essay of about 200 words presenting your view and supporting it with specific examples from your own experience, or your observations of others.

Answers will vary.

See the Writer's Workshop handout "You Be the Reader," page 107.

WRITER'S WORKSHOP HANDOUTS

FINDING THE WRITER WITHIN

Writing is putting ideas on paper. To prepare for the GED essay, practice expressing *your* ideas on paper. This activity will help.

■   **Write responses to each of the questions below. Try to answer each question quickly. Write down the first ideas that come to mind. Don't say "I don't know." Write down something on every single line.**

(1) What are three things you like about your best friend?

_____

_____

_____

(2) What are two reasons why people have pets?

_____

_____

(3) What are three disadvantages of being a millionaire?

_____

_____

_____

(4) What are two things you'd like to change about our country?

_____

_____

(5) What do you think is the biggest problem in the world today?

_____

_____

A LOOK AT THE GED ESSAY SCORING GUIDE

How will your GED essay be evaluated? What aspects of writing matter the most to the people who score the essays? The people who evaluate your GED essay will follow the guidelines given on the Scoring Guide below. To understand what the evaluators will be looking for, underline the key words and phrases that are repeated throughout the guide.

GED ESSAY SCORING GUIDE

Papers will show <u>some or all</u> of the following characteristics.

Upper-half papers make clear a definite purpose, pursued with varying degrees of effectiveness. They also have a structure that shows evidence of some deliberate planning. The writer's control of the conventions of Standard Written English (spelling, punctuation, grammar, word choice, and sentence structure) ranges from fairly reliable at 4 to confident and accomplished at 6.

6 The <u>6 paper</u> offers sophisticated ideas within an organizational framework that is clear and appropriate for the topic. The supporting statements are particularly effective because of their substance, specificity, or illustrative quality. The writing is vivid and precise, although it may contain an occasional flaw in the conventions of Standard Written English.

5 The <u>5 paper</u> is clearly organized with effective support for each of the writer's major points. While the writing offers substantive ideas, it lacks the fluency found in the 6 paper. Although there are some errors, the conventions of Standard Written English are consistently under control.

4 The <u>4 paper</u> shows evidence of the writer's organizational plan. Support, though adequate, tends to be less extensive or effective than that found in the 5 paper. The writer generally observes the conventions of Standard Written English. The errors that are present are not severe enough to interfere significantly with the writer's main purpose.

Lower-half papers either fail to convey a purpose sufficiently or lack one entirely. Consequently, their structure ranges from rudimentary at 3, to random at 2, to absent at 1. Control of the conventions of Standard Written English tends to follow this same gradient.

3 The <u>3 paper</u> usually shows some evidence of planning, although the development may be insufficient. The supporting statements may be limited to a listing or a repetition of ideas. The 3 paper often demonstrates repeated weaknesses in the conventions of Standard Written English.

2 The <u>2 paper</u> is characterized by a marked lack of organization or inadequate support for ideas. The development may be superficial or unfocused. Errors in the conventions of Standard Written English may seriously interfere with the overall effectiveness of this paper.

1 The <u>1 paper</u> lacks purpose or development. The dominant feature is the absence of control of structure or the conventions of Standard Written English. The deficiencies are so severe that the writer's ideas are difficult or impossible to understand.

NOTE: Papers which are blank, illegible, or written on a topic other than the one assigned cannot be scored, and a Writing Skills Test composite score cannot be reported.

GIVING CONSTRUCTIVE CRITICISM

When you give constructive criticism, you praise the strengths of a piece of writing. You also point out ways to improve it. Here are steps you can follow when exchanging writing with a partner.

(1) Allow enough time to read carefully and comment thoughtfully.

(2) Take turns answering the following questions:
- What examples did the writer give to support the main idea?
- What are one or two strengths of the paper?
- Was the writer's main idea easy to understand?
- What, if anything, is the biggest problem with the essay?
- What suggestions can you make to solve the problem?

(3) Always be positive—even with your criticism. Find a helpful way to say what you think.

Instead of Saying . . .	**Say . . .**
"Your spelling is unbelievably bad!"	"Your ideas are good, but the essay is sometimes hard to read because some words are misspelled."
"This sentence makes absolutely no sense."	"Can you explain what this sentence means? I don't understand it."

(4) Be specific with your comments. Point directly at the words and sentences that you enjoy, that you do not understand, or that need improvement.

Instead of Saying . . .	**Say . . .**
"You did a good job on the essay."	"You did a good job supporting the main idea of your essay."
"Some of the sentences need fixing."	"I think the second sentence is incomplete."

(5) Reread the essay after it has been revised. You'll be in a good position to see whether or not the essay has improved.

UNDERSTANDING CAUSE AND EFFECT

A GED essay topic may ask you to write about causes, or why something happens. Or you may be asked to write about the effects, or results, of something. This activity will help you understand cause and effect so that your essay will be effective.

PART ONE

■ **Complete the sentences below by giving a reason (cause) for the first part of the statement.**

(1) I am going to school because _____

(2) People need money because _____

(3) Many people do not vote because _____

(4) Knowing how to read is important because _____

PART TWO

■ **Complete the following sentences by giving a result, or effect.**

(1) Because people work, _____

(2) When a country goes to war, _____

(3) Because education is important, _____

(4) When I get hungry, _____

PART THREE

■ **For each statement, underline the cause and circle the effect.**

(1) Because it rained so hard last week, the stream overflowed.

(2) I'll send you a check so that you can buy what you need.

(3) Many people can't afford health care; as a result, they don't see a doctor often enough.

(4) Since our rent is going up, we'll be looking for a new apartment.

(5) Many people dislike paying taxes because they don't trust the government.

FREEWRITING

A fun warm-up activity to get your ideas flowing is to write continuously for a certain amount of time. This technique is called **freewriting**.

Here's an example. The writer was asked to write about why he was in school. He was given one minute to write and was told *not* to stop, even for a second. Here's what his freewriting looked like:

> *Why am I in school? Good question. Somtimes I wonder myself. I guess I think it will get me a better job so I can quit work at the warehouse. What a louzy job. I'm sick of my boss plus the jerks I work with. I'd like to work in sales. I'd be great at it. Maybe school will give me the skills I need to get my foot in the door. I'm not sure I have anything else to say about being in school. What else is there to write about? It's not a bad place. Sometimes I'd rather be home watching TV. TV takes up so much of my time but what else is their to do. Its on all day in my mothers house—its hard not to watch it.*

What good is freewriting? It's certainly *not* a technique to use during the GED essay test! However, in the weeks beforehand, as you prepare for the essay test, you may find that this activity "gets your writing in gear." Many writers use timed freewriting as a two-minute warm-up before they begin a real writing task.

■ **Practice freewriting about the topics below. Give yourself two minutes for each topic, and write *nonstop*.**

(1) music

(2) crime

IRRELEVANT IDEAS

Have you ever read a paragraph and thought, "What's this sentence in here for? It doesn't belong." In your own writing, work on including only ideas that support your main idea. Ideas that do not support the main idea are **irrelevant ideas**—ideas that do not belong.

Below is a list of ideas that a writer used to support the main idea statement *There are lots of advantages to being my age, which is twenty-three.* Which idea should not be included in the essay?

- *no more teenage stress*
- *young enough to enjoy life*
- *too many responsibilities*

- *no worries about being in the "right" social circle*
- *can get into all the nightclubs*
- *not too old to still have fun*

Did you find that the idea about having too many responsibilites should not be included? The rest of the list relates to the advantages of being twenty-three. The problem of responsibilities is a disadvantage and is therefore irrelevant to the list.

■ **Read the main idea statements and cross out the idea that should not be used in the essay.**

(1) *There are several advantages and disadvantages to being forty years old.*

- *I know a lot more now than I did five or ten years ago.*
- *more confidence*
- *wish I made more money*
- *too old to stay out late*

- *life is settled, steady*
- *I fear middle age will slow me down*
- *fear of death*

(2) *There is too much advertising on television today.*

- *interruptions are annoying*
- *makes kids want everything they see*

- *most ads are really dumb*
- *dogfood ads are pretty entertaining*

(3) *Our biggest problem today is children living in poverty.*

- *undernourished*
- *many are being raised by drug addicts*
- *don't spend enough time playing safely*

- *poorly educated*
- *the elderly have problems too*

ANSWERING THE TOPIC QUESTION

In this activity you'll practice writing a one-sentence answer to the question asked in a GED writing topic. Your answer can be used as your main idea statement, and it will help you focus clearly on the topic. Here is an example.

> "It's a terrible shame that young people spend so much of their time staring at television. If we unplugged all the television sets, our children would grow up to be healthier, better educated, and more independent."
>
> Do you agree or disagree with this statement? Write an essay of about 200 words presenting your point of view and supporting it with specific examples from your own experience or your observations of others.

Here are some ways to answer the question asked.

- *I agree with the statement that it is a shame that children watch so much television.*
- *Children watching television is not such a bad thing.*
- *Television and children should not mix.*
- *The statement that children should not watch so much TV is right on target.*

■ **Write a one-sentence answer to the question asked in each topic below.**

> It seems that more and more Americans are exercising and watching what they eat. What do you think is causing this "fitness kick"? Is it primarily concern with health, body image, or something else? Write an essay of about 200 words that tells the causes of the "fitness kick" and gives examples.

> What qualities do you think make up a good employer? Some people believe honesty is important; others believe that flexibility is.
>
> Write an essay of about 200 words that identifies the qualities you think a good employer has, giving specific examples to back up your ideas.

WRITER'S WORKSHOP

SHOW, DON'T TELL

Practice adding examples, details, and specific ideas to show the reader what you mean. Remember that the more specific you are, the easier it will be for your reader to understand your point of view.

PART ONE

■ **Read each statement below; then fill in the blanks with an example that shows the reader what the statement means. Be sure to write in complete sentences.**

(1) Many people work at night instead of during the day. For example, _____

_____

(2) The best thing about education is _____. For example, _____

_____

(3) Higher taxes are a _____ idea. For example, _____

_____

PART TWO

■ **Add examples and specific ideas to this paragraph. Make the writing come alive for the reader.**

A good friend is fun to be with. She should try to make you happy when you're around her. In addition, a good friend should be concerned about you. She should try to understand your feelings and help you.

_____

_____

_____

_____

_____

_____

PULLING APART RUN-ON SENTENCES

A **run-on sentence** is two or more sentences joined together incorrectly. Avoid writing run-on sentences on your GED essay. They make it hard for a reader to understand what you're trying to say. One way to correct a run-on sentence is to separate the run-together sentences with a period.

Run-Ons

It's better to tell the truth lies will always harm you in the end.
It's better to tell the truth, lies will always harm you in the end.

Correction

It's better to tell the truth. Lies will always harm you in the end.

To check your essay for run-ons, read each sentence slowly, on its own. Remember that a comma is not enough to join two complete sentences together.

■ **If a sentence is a run-on, correct it on the lines below.**

(1) Getting an education is my most important goal, and it takes a lot of effort.

_____

(2) Three things really annoy me, being disloyal to friends is one of them.

_____

(3) One time, my teacher showed me an easier way to take notes, this helped me a lot.

_____

(4) Giving kids chores is important for example even emptying a trash can helps kids to be responsible.

_____

ADDING CONNECTING WORDS TO RUN-ON SENTENCES

Many times, a run-on sentence can be fixed by joining the run-together sentences with a connecting word.

Run-On

A spouse should always listen, he should try to understand as much as possible.

Correction

A spouse should always listen, **and** he should try to understand as much as possible.

Run-On

A guy on drugs will commit crimes, he doesn't have regard for the law.

Correction

A guy on drugs will commit crimes **because** he doesn't have regard for the law.

Below are some connecting words commonly used to join sentences. If you come across a run-on sentence in your writing, try correcting it with one of these words.

and	*if*	*when*	*because*	*for example*
so	*therefore*	*then*	*but*	*in addition*

■ **Revise the following paragraph by correcting all run-on sentences. Try to use the connecting words in the box above as much as possible.**

Computers are changing the way kids learn, it can be a scary thing. Little children are learning what computers can do my three-year-old niece has one in her nursery school. What has happened to working on the basics before we move to complex things like a computer? Parents are asking questions, no one is answering. It is as if people are saying computers are here to stay, we will use them to teach our children. Many do not agree with this philosophy many prefer the traditional methods.

SENTENCE FRAGMENTS

To be complete, a sentence must

- have a subject
- have a verb
- express a complete thought

If a group of words lacks one or more of these elements, it is called a **sentence fragment**, or an incomplete sentence.

> **Sentence fragments**
>
> The most alarming story in the paper today. (no verb)
> Paid for it with his life. (no subject)
> When I was a lot younger. (no complete thought)

■ **Decide which of the following are complete sentences. If a group of words is a sentence fragment, correct it by adding words of your own.**

(1) Decked out in the finest jewels. ————————————————————

(2) A father should be there for his children. ————————————————

(3) A good friend in Washington, D.C. ————————————————————

(4) Because things are never easy. ——————————————————————

(5) Went back to get her high school degree. ——————————————

(6) Thinking ahead is a wise strategy for success. ————————————

(7) Whenever they saw each other. ————————————————————————

(8) For example, the most obvious reason. ————————————————

SENTENCE FRAGMENTS IN A PARAGRAPH

Can you spot the sentence fragment in this paragraph?

Having a pet can really change a person's life in a positive way. Unlike people, animals listen to you and support you no matter what. They never have plans of their own, and they are completely devoted. Older people tend to enjoy pets. Because the elderly need companionship. Having a pet can make life a little more peaceful and comforting.

Did you find the sentence fragment *Because the elderly need companionship*? You may have had trouble finding it because it makes sense when read with the sentence that comes before it. To correct the fragment, join it to the preceding sentence, which it belongs with.

Older people tend to enjoy pets. ~~*Because*~~ **because** *the elderly need companionship.*

■ **Find and correct each sentence fragment by connecting it to a complete sentence or adding words.**

(1) *The voting age in our country should be raised to at least twenty-one. People younger than this really don't have any idea what is going on. They are not ready to make decisions for our country. Because they can barely make good decisions for themselves. Electing government officials. Is serious business. We should not take it lightly. Or our country will fall.*

(2) *The person who has had the most influence on me is my oldest brother. He was the one who practically raised me. When my mother died and my dad was never around. A great guy. Always there when I needed him. Without my brother, I never would have gotten this job I have. He knew my boss and put in a good word for me.*

COMMONLY MISSPELLED WORDS

There are several words that, because they sound like other common words, are often misspelled. The list below is far from complete. If you know of other words that you have spelled incorrectly in the past, add them to this list. As you prepare to take the GED Writing Skills Test, review this list.

there they're (they are) their	**There** is a reason for this bad behavior. **They're** planning to protest his decision. **Their** ideas are worth listening to.
to two too (also)	We want **to** make our position clear. There are **two** sides to every issue. The public agrees with us **too**.
your you're (you are)	Explain **your** opinion on the human rights issue. It appears that **you're** changing your mind.
its it's (it is)	The committee has reversed **its** decision before. **It's** a trickier issue than we had realized earlier.
whose who's (who is, who has)	**Whose** opinion is the most informed? We have a right to know **who's** paying the bill.

■ **Read the paragraph below, paying particular attention to spelling. Cross out any mistakes and insert the correct word just as you would on the GED test.**

The person whose most influential in my life right now is my wife. There are to things that she has done for me that have changed me forever. First of all, she taught me whose in charge of my life—me. Before I met my wife, I believed my life was running it's course no matter what I did. Now I know I can be whatever I want to be and that she'll stand by me too. Secondly, my wife helped me figure out what skills I had. Let's face it, if you don't think you have any skills, your not going to get anywhere.

> ### Topic
>
> What characteristics do you look for when you are searching for a good job? Write an essay of about 200 words presenting your view and supporting it with specific examples from your own experience, or your observations of others.

On the following pages are six sample GED essays. To get a better understanding of how readers will judge *your* essay, judge some other students' writing.

(1) Read *all six* essays. Do not write or take any notes on them.

(2) Remove the papers and put them in numerical order, with *1* being the *least* effective essay and *6* being the *most* effective. Take about 10 to 12 minutes to do this. Use the Scoring Guide on page 83 to make your evaluations.

(3) When you have finished putting the papers in order, turn to pages 121 and 122 to read the scores and commentary that GED readers might give the essays.

(4) Do your scores match those of the sample readers? If not, read the commentary again, and try to see why each paper was scored the way it was.

(5) Now take the essay you wrote on page 74 for the Post-Test. Using the scoring guide, decide what score you might receive for your essay. Try evaluating a partner's essay as well.

My characterishcs I seek in a job are basic things people enjoy looking for. Easy to get along co-workers, somewhat good pay, opportunities for promotion.

For example some jobs you have you don't enjoy working at because the people you work with are just not happy, nice, easy to talk to. When you first start a job you want to be able to talk to your co-workers. And ask them adevise. Second you need a job with some pay so you could at least see some of the money you work for. I'am not saying a lot of pay but at least more then $3.35 an hour. Last but not least, you need some type of opportunities for promotion. If you are not going to get rewarded for your hard work you are not going to stay very long.

These few things are my characteristics that I would like in a job I choice.

In looking for a good job, one must consider many important aspects. In order to make a decision for myself, I just look for what my future potential will be in the long run. Will I be able to advance? Will I be able to grow?

Other things to think about are benefits. Does this job offer any medical or dental plans? Who is going to pay for these bills? If my employer does than I'm in in better shape.

How about retirement? This is important, because we all want ~~piece~~ peace of mind knowing that when we have worked for someone long enough, we can relax and enjoy life to the fullest.

~~Above all~~, I would still consider advancement the most important. Look at the man who started as a floor sweeper for Boeing Aircraft, and is now president of the company. ~~It's~~ possible.

When I look for a job, I look for what the company has to offer. Currently, I'm a diesel technician for a large Ford heavy truck dealership. Things such as working conditions, the top mechanics pay, the existence of a union, and the type of insurance coverage offered are of primary interest to me.

Working ~~conditions~~ conditions vary from shop to shop. Some garages are ankle-deep in grease and have tools strewn everywhere you look. The ideal environment to me is a clean, well-kept work area with good tools available and kept in an orderly manner. All these things will make my job much easier, and will make me more money. The less time I spend wandering around looking for the right tool, the ~~most~~ more ~~money~~ money I will make.

If I walk into a shop and find the top mechanic's base pay rate is high, I know there is room for advancement. If the rate is only slightly higher than that of a beginner, I know I'll soon have to start looking for another job.

If the shop is run by a union, I can feel reasonably sure that the equipment is modern and is in safe working condition. The union shops usually have more equipment and the latest tools available for their mechanics. After all, using the latest tools and gadgets is half the fun of being a mechanic.

When I'm ready to look for a new job, the company must meet my standards. They must ~~have~~ have a good pay and ~~some~~ benifit plan. The shop must be neat and clean, with all of the tools essential for me to do my job. Usually, I try to stay with ~~union~~ union shops. They almost always meet these standards.

Characteristics are important when seeking a job. People consider good pay. Good working hours with flexiability is important for others. Benifits and vaction policies interest ~~some~~ some skill workers. Opportuincies and promotions are also intportant in a good job.

Characteristices are important when seeking a good job. Often people get injured and have no benefits or insurance. Promotion helps with pay raise, and higher rank in jobs. Pay may help someone with ~~his~~ his family or other things. Liberal vacation policies give time to spend with love ones, or to travel.

SAMPLE ESSAY E

When applying for a job, the first thing I look for is what kind of a job it is. Working for a fast food isn't something I want to do. From past experiences I wouldn't want that kind of job again, because when I did you give the job all you have and they take advantage of you. I worked every week, 4-5 days a week, and didn't get $50.00 in each paycheck. They help the ones they like and the others they just let do whatever. Like us cashiers, we couldn't get a raise until the supervisor got his bonus from the head of the company.

The second thing is the pay. Minimum wage isn't going to help you with anything. You don't get enough money to really do the things you want to do or go the places you want to go. It just gives you some spending money. If you have car payments or insurance payments, you couldn't do it on minimum wage. I now get $4.35/hr. and that helps out a little more, but I don't really get the hours to make enough money for what I need to do.

Which brings me to the next topic: where the job is and how many hours I'll be getting. If the job is to far from my house I'm not going to want to go there if I'm not getting at least 16-20 hrs at no less than $4.00 - $4.50 per hour, because I'll be spending most of my pay on gas or public transportation. I would like the job to be fairly close to my house if I can get it, but if not I've learned to take what I can get.

A good job for myself would be able to play NBA Basketball. Considering all the money I could make by doing something that I won't mind playing for free. By plaing for NBA you get chance to go on tripe and I love going on trip. you make any where around $2,000,000,000 to $980,000,000 a year so the pay is good. It's good to enjoy enjoy your work or job and I love playing basket ball, ever since grade school to college I love the game of basket ball so it would be a honer for me. The chance are thin because there are millions of Basket Ball players, but only 23 NBA Teams, and there are only 13 men to a team so figer that a rough 299 people out of million. One day I will be one of them highly pay player.

SAMPLE ESSAY A / SCORE: 3

The main idea in the introductory paragraph hints at a clear plan of development and structure. It seems as if each of three characteristics will be explained in its own paragraph in the body. However, the writer fails to follow through on this plan. In addition, the first two sentences are awkwardly phrased.

The essay would have been considerably stronger if it had been more fully developed, with each of the three characteristics explained in detail. However, this alone would probably not have been enough to earn a higher score, because the essay also contains a sentence fragment, and there are several other lapses in usage and mechanics.

Overall, the essay leaves the impression of an effort in which some structure is apparent but not realized and in which the writing itself is neither clear nor under control.

SAMPLE ESSAY B / SCORE: 4

This essay has a clear structure. It begins with an introduction that has a main idea—i.e., "one must consider many important aspects"; it explains the main idea in the body paragraphs that follow; and it has a conclusion that sums up a point earlier made. Within this structure, the writing is clear and under control. Though there is an occasional lapse in usage and mechanics, the writer generally communicates clearly and directly.

Though this essay is not especially well developed, the main idea is adequately supported. Essays earning a score of 4 do so not by virtue of their length but by virtue of their control of organization and structure. Moreover, there is a clear difference in substance between essays at the 3 and 4 levels. The concluding example of Sample Essay B illustrates an example of substance.

SAMPLE ESSAY C / SCORE: 6

This essay has a strong introduction. It begins with a general statement—"When I look for a job, I look for what the company has to offer"—and then provides a clear context for the generalization—working for a Ford dealership. This specific example is followed by a clear main idea statement.

By grounding the discussion of job characteristics in his current job at the dealership, the writer makes it possible to provide highly specific—and therefore effective—details in support of the main idea. The excellent development makes the essay convincing and interesting, and the writing throughout is clear, forceful, and precise.

SAMPLE ESSAY D / SCORE: 2

This essay lacks adequate planning and development. Though the first sentence might be the start of a main idea, the essay does not go on to clarify or support the idea. In fact, notice that the first sentence of paragraph 2 is almost the same as the first sentence of paragraph 1.

The essay repeats ideas instead of explaining them. The sentence structure—while "correct"—is also repetitious. The repetition gives the impression of a series of mechanical and superficial responses to the topic. The essay is further weakened by the lapses in the use of verbs.

SAMPLE ESSAY E / SCORE: 5

Though this essay lacks a formal introductory paragraph, the essay is well structured. Each of the three paragraphs begins with a statement of a characteristic followed by a series of details showing why the characteristic is important. For example, the account in paragraph 2 of the writer's experience in a fast-food restaurant clearly illustrates what she means by "Working for fast food isn't something I want to do."

Often, what distinguishes a level 5 essay from a level 4 is the amount of detail the writer provides in support of the main idea. Level 5 essays usually include examples that are particularly effective because of their specificity. Sample Essay E has good, specific examples.

SAMPLE ESSAY F / SCORE: 1

This essay has a clear main idea, but it lacks the structure necessary to support the main idea effectively. Instead of focusing on the characteristics of a good job, the writer focuses on his love of basketball. In addition, the writer's difficulty with usage and mechanics further weakens the effort. The awkwardly phrased first sentence is followed by a sentence fragment, and the essay contains numerous lapses in good sentence structure and spelling.